Okay is not enough: Steps To Achieve Goals that (you may assume) are Out of Your Reach

The Greatest Danger For Most Of Us Isn't That Our Aim Is Too High And Miss It, But That It Is Too Low And We Reach It.

Rose Croix

Table of Contents

Introduction

Writing down goals isn't necessarily a panacea for magically attaining them. In fact, goal setting can be a source of frustration and self-berating for many people, and as such, those beautiful goals and dreams end up in dusty old journals that are seldom opened.

What is it about goals that make them so difficult to attain? Why do we, in a moment of zest, dream up the most amazing goals, yet find it difficult to commit to them? Is it a result of faulty methods we have been taught, a lack of the willingness to apply the methods, or a combination of both?

In order to answer these and many more questions, this book has been written to help you identify the things that sabotage your efforts towards the attainment of your goals. There is no room for theorizing about goal setting; you, of all people, must have probably "been there, done that!" The focus of this book is purely practical; action steps that are sure to yield the result you so dearly seek.

As much as I would love to say the techniques and tips shared in this book work 100% of the time, I cannot promise you that all your goals will be attained simply by reading this book. However, I can absolutely guarantee that if you diligently commit to following the methods and apply them religiously, you will have tremendous results that will make your previous achievements look like child's play! The techniques contained in this book are capable of increasing your productivity and success in tenfold (or 10x in modern language).

People give up on their goals because it is easier to maintain the status quo of their lives. So, they naturally (is that even naturally?) avoid the expected "difficult" requirements for improving their lives beyond where it currently is. This is true for many as they have lesser motivation for achieving their dreams than they have for losing what is already theirs. This is why many people are stuck with a standard they have come to accept, rather than stretching themselves to attain a version of themselves which they have envisioned.

If your day seems to fly by leaving you achieving less than half of what you set out to, or if your goals (short, medium, and long-term) seem like a tale that was once told in a distant land, or if you just lack the self-confidence and motivation to push through, then this book will help to set forth an exact plan of action that will bring you clarity and help you attain those goals that seem beyond your reach.

So, go ahead, dust off that old goal book of yours and breathe life back into your desires with the lessons you will learn in this easy-to-comprehend and fun-filled book. I'll suggest you adopt an attitude of fun while you read and apply these positive life-altering lessons. Being too serious about it will tire you out too soon. Working towards your goals is a herculean task by itself; why would you want to add to that too much seriousness? Relax; be flexible without losing focus on why you are learning what you are learning.

And as Ted Turner, the media mogul and philanthropist, says, *"You should set goals beyond your reach so you always have something to live for."*

Chapter 1: Finding Your Purpose

"It's not enough to have lived. We should be determined to live for something." (Winston S. Churchill, 1874 – 1965; British Prime Minister, Author, and Orator)

More Than Mere Survival

The twig floats down the river going with the flow of the current. It pauses not because it wants to but because something is blocking its path. With enough push from the river's current, it overcomes the obstacle and continues down the river. It has no purpose, no direction, except where the river wills it to go. It simply drifts according to the whims and caprices of the river, never daring to go upstream or against the river's current.

Does that describe you in some ways? If it does, well, it's not a death sentence. The fact that you are reading this book shows that you are willing to take back control of your life. You no longer want to be driven by the "river" of life but to know exactly why you do what you do and to be able to change what you are doing if the reason doesn't satisfy you.

Drifters don't know their purpose – not that they don't have one, they simply don't know it. So, they "settle." And they "survive." Technically, there's nothing wrong with settling and surviving, except that it equates you with lower mammals. Do you see how monkeys or lions set out every morning in search of something to keep them alive? Well, that's how drifters are; "let's just stay alive." That's called existing. Michael Jackson, one of the world's greatest pop musicians, admonished "*stop existing and start living,*" (Heal The World, 1991).

In order to achieve anything meaningful in life, you must be willing to go beyond mere survival; you must be willing to wake up from drifting and floating aimlessly. But how do you wake up? How do you get yourself out of the humdrum of just mere survival? Here's how. Ask yourself:

- What is the reason for my survival?

- To what end?

- What is the essence of waking up every morning and doing what I do?

This line of self-questioning opens you up to start digging deep into yourself to discover your purpose.

More Questions

What Inspires Me?

Another way to ask this question is: what makes me come alive? This question shifts your focus to seek that which you are passionate about. When something makes you come alive, it brings out your creative abilities, time stops for you when you are doing it, and you never see it as a bore or a chore. Your purpose inspires you to go beyond mere survival to committing to a cause that is bigger than you. Martin Luther King Jr. connected to a cause bigger than survival when he said: "*I have a dream!*"

What Are My Strengths?

If you've never heard the expression, "being in your element," do not fret, you are not alone. But it doesn't have anything to do with chemistry – I never really liked chemistry too you know. There are some things you are naturally gifted, talented, or good at. You handle them with so much ease other people wonder how you do it. There are other things you have passion for even though you may not be naturally gifted or talented in that area. Now, here's what's magical about this: when your talent and passion meet it is known as your element! Being in your element means you are using your strengths in the most efficient and effective way. In other words, you are combining your talents with your passion which equals unstoppable strength from within.

To find your inborn strength, begin to ask questions like: am I more inclined to rebel against the norm and come up with a different perspective? Do I usually think outside the box? Do I see opportunities and patterns where others see difficulty and complexity? Am I a naturally gifted orator, communicator, change agent, leader, or technocrat? Am I excellent at handling minute details when executing projects? These questions will uncover your talent and passion and show you where your element lies.

In What Way Do I Give The Highest Value?

If your talent and passion are not in alignment, then you may find yourself doing something that you don't like even though you are good at it or being passionate about something even though you really don't have the talent. In that case, you are not adding the highest value you can possibly add. You are giving what doesn't really sit well with you. Start looking at the problems that you really enjoy solving; that is the key to finding where you can deliver the highest possible value. Marrying that with what you are naturally good at makes you the definition of success.

Stop Drifting

There are many people who were drifters for a very long time before discovering their purpose. Do you feel slighted by the term "drifter?" Here are two good examples of people who were drifters at a point in their lives but who later went on to discover their purpose and changed their lives for good.

1. Morgan Freeman drifted for 50 years of his life before becoming a world respected actor, film director, narrator, and philanthropist. He spent his early years chasing a career as a fighter pilot in the Air Force. But he had an epiphany which made it clear to him that he was only in love with the idea of being a pilot, but not in love with the job itself. He quit the Air Force in 1959 and continued drifting until he went back to something he did in his childhood days, acting!

2. Harland David Sanders, better known as Colonel Sanders of Kentucky Fried Chicken (KFC) drifted until he was into his 40s. Because his father died and left him with two younger siblings, he was forced to fend for them. He cooked meals for them and quickly developed his talent for cooking delicious meals. He left home when his mother remarried and drifted from one job to another. He didn't make any significant progress until he went back to something he did during his childhood, cooking. Even after his business closed down at the age of 66, he went about franchising his secret chicken

recipe and eventually became the world's largest fast-food chicken chain.

Am I suggesting that you have to drift for more than half your life before you find your purpose? Certainly not! I am sure you are aware of people who found their life purpose at an early age. Mark Zuckerberg of Facebook is a typical example. So, your age doesn't really matter when it comes to finding your purpose. And by the way, you do not have to make a world-renown discovery or accomplishment before you are applauded as someone who has found his or her purpose. Your purpose is meant to give you personal fulfillment first and foremost. It doesn't matter if you are recognized or acknowledged by any other person or not. As long as it gives you a genuine reason to step out and face a new challenge each day, your purpose will make you more likely to find a way around any challenge that comes your way.

Here's a quick food for thought as we round up this chapter. "Don't ask yourself what the world needs. Ask yourself what makes you come alive, and go do that, because what the world needs is people who have come alive." (Howard Thurman, 1899 – 1981; African-American Author, Educator, Theologian, and Civil Rights Leader)

Chapter 2: Going Beyond the Paycheck

"The two most important days in your life are the day you are born and the day you find out why." *(Mark Twain, 1835 – 1910; American Writer and Entrepreneur)*

If you have a job or you do any kind of work to earn a living, you should be used to goals like, *"I'll like to double my income in the coming year!"* I am going to take a wild guess and assume that you probably didn't double your income. I know this because it happens to almost all of us. But why is that? Why do we set amazing goals and fail to meet them no matter how noble our intentions were?

Here's the thing with many people; they assume that the reason they work is for the monetary reward. And that assumption makes them set their sights on the wrong target. But isn't the paycheck a good enough reason? Do you need to find any other purpose for doing what you do beyond the money? Well, if you think you're doing what you do for money, ask yourself, *"Why do I want the money?"* Perhaps that will begin to give you insights into what's more important for you – what truly drives you.

It could be that you want to make enough money so

that you quit your job and spend more quality time with the people you love. It could be that you want to have the freedom to travel and see distant lands and places. It could also be that you want to give your family the lifestyle of their dreams. You see, money isn't the primary reason or the purpose why you do what you do; money is just a means to what you want.

Let us assume for a minute that your boss is going to pay you an additional $100 if you put in extra work on Saturday when you are supposed to be with your family and friends. The cash may be good but it may not be enough motivation especially if you have something very important to do during the weekend. You'll probably have to weigh your options before making a decision. But if your child is in critical health and you urgently need an additional $100 for his or her treatment, you wouldn't think twice before jumping at any opportunity to earn that money. That is if you are a good parent (of which I am willing to bet my left kidney that you are!).

Can you see the difference now? Both situations involved money, but one didn't have enough motivation to push you to immediate action while the other had you up and going in an instant. The situation involved the same amount of money but different reactions. Why? There is a clear purpose – a "why" – beyond the paycheck in the second situation.

Note: *If you are trying to make enough money so that you can quit your job, it shows that you are not finding fulfillment in that job. You have "settled" for* *something you don't like and you are merely surviving. Don't quit your job simply by reading this book; no, not yet. But shift your focus from seeing the job as annoying and begin to see it as a stepping stone to your dream. That way, you are not frustrated but appreciative and eager for something better!*

Take this lesson and begin to apply it to your life right now. You'll discover you have more reasons to get out of bed every morning to accomplish what you need to accomplish to fulfill your purpose. If you find a good enough reason why you should "*double your income in the coming year*" then you are more likely to achieve that goal or at least come close to achieving it. Without finding that reason, that purpose, or that motivation, I'm afraid your goal of making more money will simply end up in the pages of your awesome looking goal book!

"*Be grateful for what you already have while you pursue your goals. If you aren't grateful for what you already have, what makes you think you would be happy with more.*" (Roy T. Bennett; Author)

Willpower alone cannot provide enough motivation to pull you through. You need that underlying reason in order to keep you going even in the face of adversity. "*Forget about willpower. It's time for why-power. Your choices are only meaningful when you connect them to your desires and dreams. The wisest and most motivating choices are the ones aligned with that which you identify as your purpose, your core self, and your highest values. You've got to want something, and know why you want it, or you'll end up giving up too easily."* (Darren Hardy; American Author, Motivational Speaker, and former Publisher of Success Magazine)

Chapter 3: Nail the "Why" And the "How" Will Show Up

"He who has a 'why' to live for can bear almost any 'how.'" (Friedrich Nietzsche, 1844 – 1900; German Philosopher)

Important things in life like finding your purpose are difficult to accomplish, right? Wrong! True, there are several paths that can lead to the discovery of your purpose or your "why," but it certainly isn't as difficult as you may think.

Here's a simple process you can follow to figure out what your "why" is.

Go Deep… Go Deeper

Take some time to think about what it is you really want. When you have that clearly in your mind, write it down on a piece of paper or in your personal journal and then ask yourself what about it is important to you.

For example, if you have determined that losing

weight is what you really want at this point in your life:

First step: write that down and ask: *"What about losing weight is important to me?"*

Now here comes the tricky part. Something will definitely pop into your mind, but the trickery in it is that we (almost all humans) have the tendency to self-edit. So you are most likely to edit the first thing that comes into your mind to make it sound perfect. Stop it! You don't have to self-edit. First of all, no one is going to inspect your journal to see if you were right or wrong. There is no right or wrong in this matter. Simply write down what comes to your mind without trying too hard to make it sound perfect. It may be something like, *"so that I will have a sexy body."* Whatever it is, just write it down.

Next step: put that reason into the first question. Like this, *"What about having a sexy body is important to me?"* Do you see the logic? You are digging deep... and deeper. The answer to that might be, *"to boost my self-image."*

Next step: repeat the loop with whatever answer you get. *"What about boosting your self-image is important to you?"*

It will be a good practice if you can go down seven levels deep, all the while answering honestly. You will discover at the core of your beliefs lies the real reason – the "why" – behind your goal of losing weight (or whatever your goal happens to be).

You may discover that:

- You want to lose weight not just because you want to keep fit but because deep down you want to be valued for who you really are.

- You are looking to work from home not just because you want to be your own boss or because you want a more flexible schedule but because it allows you to be more creative in the delivery of what is buried deep inside of you without being boxed in by a job.

- You want to make more money not simply because you like counting cash but because you are trying to overcome a deep sense of insecurity.

And the list goes on!

Go deep... and deeper, and you will find things that are beyond your base-level motivations. Once you find that one thing that is the "why" behind what you want, keep it constantly on your mind. Remind yourself about it daily and as often as you can throughout your day. You will suddenly gain more clarity and feel more motivated to speak and act from deep within instead of acting from your head. You will be driven by that one reason to connect more with people and things around you; to be more truthful and honest in your dealings; to become more powerful and successful.

You will gain insights to achieve goals that appeared

difficult because the "how" (the ways) will show up out of your commitment to the "why." Your optimal performance will come to the fore because you are driven by something from your core.

So, grab a pen and paper right now and stop reading this book until you dig deep enough to discover your why. Are you still reading? C'mon! Go dig up your "why!"

Chapter 4: Throw Your Weight

Behind Your Choices

"Drifters allow the world to write the story of their lives. They let mechanisms of reward and punishment — pats on the head, fear, the easiness of an option — to determine what they do." (Ruth Chang; Philosopher)

One of the reasons why many people have not discovered their purpose is because they see it as a difficult choice between two or several options and they naturally fear to make hard choices since it is usually an occasion for agonizing. I mean, of all the several possible "whys" available, how on God's green earth would you just pick one and make it your purpose for whatever it is that you do? That type of mental activity is rather too difficult for many people so they simply drift along with life and accept whatever is shoved down their throats and settle for a mediocre life.

But what if there was a way to actually make so-called difficult choices a lot less difficult? What if the challenge of thinking your way into finding a purpose is a blessing in disguise?

Okay, let's remove the disguise from the blessing and see what we can make of it. Look at it this way: easy choices are easy because one of the options is better than the other. Difficult choices are difficult because none of the choices are completely better than the other. But we are used to making choices that are easy since we can clearly see the glaring overall advantage of one option over the other. However, that will keep us as mental slaves to reasons presented to us by the options. You will no longer have the opportunity to exercise your normative powers.

So, in simple terms, making a difficult choice is a way to create your own reasons to make your choice the right one for you. It is seizing the opportunity to put your creative abilities to work; to throw your full weight behind a decision and make that decision right. You are not simply accepting a reason handed to you by the options; rather, you are creating a reason from deep within you. You are tapping into your creative reserves to discover who you really are. You are not allowing external situations to write your life's story. Reward or punishment no longer dictates what you do.

How To Make Difficult Decisions

You do not have to be right or wrong when finding your purpose because it definitely isn't a matter of being correct or not.

Here's what you need to do:

1. Realize that the decision before you isn't quantifiable like you would do with things like weight, mass, or length. Understand that you are dealing with values that are not scientifically measured. So, do not measure the value of your decisions by the same comparisons you would apply to physical properties. For example, the weights of two objects are either the same, or one is heavier or lighter than the other. But that does not apply to things like kindness, beauty, and they certainly do not apply to your purpose.

2. Take a trip back into your past. Your purpose or purposes have a way of showing up in several places throughout your life especially during your childhood. They impact you in a way that they will always remain fresh in your memory. Remember stories we looked at in chapter 1? Morgan Freeman and Colonel Sanders had something in their childhood that held the key to their "whys." Recount about 10 to 12 stories that impacted you from your past to a friend who is willing to help you discover your "why" and you will be amazed at the things that stand out. These things will get you closer to finding your purpose and help you make the decision you need to make.

3. Throw your full weight behind your purpose. Own it! Put your agency behind your choice

and refuse to be limited by structures like gender, social class, customs, ethnicity, religion, or even ability.

4. Share your "why" with as many people as you can. This will help you to continuously refine your purpose. Remember, your purpose is not about being right or wrong. It is subject to continuous refinement. And as you share your "why" with other people, you will also inspire them to move beyond the mundane to something bigger than them. Plus, if by any chance, someone happens to ask what you do, you can go ahead and share your "why" with them instead simply stating what you do. For example, "*I love seeing the joy in parent's faces when their kids perform well in school. That is why I teach with so much passion.*" This is more inspiring than simply saying, "*I am a teacher.*"

So, just in case you haven't figured out your "why" or you skipped the closing exercise in the previous chapter, here's your second chance at discovering your purpose. Don't worry; no one is going to judge you for being right or wrong. You can always work on it as your life unfolds.

Chapter 5: Crossing The Limits of Success

"Plateaus are a manifestation of the law of diminishing returns, and when we reach one it simply means that it is time to adjust our methods." (Chris Matakas, Author, Owner and Lead Instructor at Matakas Brazilian Jiu-Jitsu Academy)

Attaining success is good – it does feel great! However, the problem with attaining success for most people is that they tend to plateau after reaching their goals. You see, setting goals and attaining them is one thing, surpassing the limits you set for yourself is a different ballgame entirely. No matter how high you aim when setting your goals, you are only setting a limit for yourself. Not that there is anything bad in setting goals except that when you attain them, you have reached a limit. It is up to you to either settle at that plateau or to break the limits of that success and use that achievement as a springboard that will launch you into greater heights.

It is a mistake to think that only people who are stuck in an unsatisfactory job are the ones afraid to leave their comfort zone. You can be a successful author, entrepreneur, artist, chef, athlete, or whatever it is you are and still get stuck in your comfort zone in spite of your success. For you to continue to be an achiever, you must keep moving and never settle. "*Achievers move forward at all times. Achievement is not a plateau, it's a beginning.*" (Ziad K. Abdelnour; *Economic Warfare: Secrets of Wealth Creation in the Age of Welfare Politics, 2011.*)

I am not suggesting that you won't get to plateaus in your climb to success. Every once in a while you will hit plateaus but the key is not to settle at the plateaus. But then, how do you go beyond peaks of achievements? How do you not settle? How do you keep the motivation going?

It's quite simple: it is by keeping an eye on your motivation to know when you are drifting from focusing on approaching challenges to concentrating on avoiding mistakes.

Approaching versus Avoiding

A bird in the hand is worth two in the bush, right? Well, this is the main ingredient when you are cooking a recipe for a plateauing dish. It will taste really good in your mouth but will give you a tummy ache!

The mentality of protecting what you have achieved instead of risking it in a quest for getting more will always keep you in a state of non-forward movement. It will keep you operating from a fear-based mindset. This is known as the avoid-orientation. Your progress in your professional or personal life is halted because you are focused on avoiding risks and anything that will jeopardize your achievements already recorded. You are essentially playing it safe; shifting from "why" to "what." In order words, avoid-orientation is all about maintaining the status quo. This is why many people only have hopes and dreams and their dreams are merely that – dreams! As soon as they encounter any challenge, they revert back to their current lifestyle.

On the other hand, approach-orientation is focusing on the rewards in spite of the risks involved; fear of failing or making mistakes doesn't stop you. *"If you are not prepared to be wrong, you'll never come up with anything original."* (Sir Ken Robinson, British Author, Speaker, and International Advisor)

Your goal is to keep moving forward – being satisfied with your progress but eager for more.

Avoiding makes you hold on to past glory; approaching keeps you reaching for new heights and glory.

Avoiding makes you lose your identity; approaching keeps you refining your identity.

Avoiding keeps you holding on to someone you used to be; approaching keeps you proactively becoming the person of your dreams.

"I firmly believe you never should spend your time being the former anything." (Condoleezza Rice, 66th US Secretary of State)

If you're like most people, you'll hit a plateau somewhere along your personal or professional journey (that is, if you're not already resting in the cozy nest of a plateau!). It's okay to get to that place but what is not okay is to stay in that place unless of course, you have given up on further progress.

Chapter 6: The End-Game Illusion

"I'm different than most people. When I cross the finish line of a big race, I see that people are ecstatic, but I'm thinking about what I'm going to do tomorrow. It's as if my journey is everlasting, and there is no finish line." (David Goggins; Veteran US Navy SEAL, American Ultra-marathon Runner, Motivational Speaker, Author)

If only you could hit the $200k per year goal; if only you could shed those extra pounds; if that particular person could be your significant other... then you'll live happily ever after! Well, that's how it feels from the bottom of the mountain. But when you climb to that level, it's just another springboard from where life will nudge you forward. If you heed the nudge, you will set a new end-game; if you pay deaf ears, you will plateau. It's that simple.

No matter your level of success, there is still something extra that needs to be done. There's never going to be a point where you'll have nothing more to aspire to. It is an error to assume like Alexander the Great said, *"There are no more worlds to conquer!"* Whether the story is true or not is debatable, but if only Alexander could look just a little bit beyond his so-called final conquest, he would have seen that there were an infinite number of worlds he hadn't yet conquered. And I know that you know I am not referring to one long-dead monarch called Alexander! Your current level of success is not the final conquest; there's still more to be done.

The idea of a finish line is merely an illusion. Reaching your current goals is not the end of your journey. There simply is no finish line; there is only progress. This is why when you stop progressing, you lose a sense of purpose and happiness eludes you. "*Without continual growth and progress, such words as improvement, achievement, and success have no meaning.*" (Benjamin Franklin, 1706 – 1790; One of US Founding Fathers and Polymath)

If you rush yourself into meeting a supposed finish line, you are more likely to get frustrated at your success and even life in general.

Learn a lesson or two from Buzz Aldrin, one of the first humans to walk on the moon. After that height of success, he became an alcoholic and had to battle depression. Why? Plateau, finish line, end-game illusion! It's like, "*I've reached my peak and there are no more worlds to conquer!*" After all, what else is there to achieve after walking on the moon?

Have you wondered what happened to William "The Refrigerator" Perry? This is a man who pulled through negative self-talk and insecurities about his body weight to become a world-renowned athlete. He was so famous he had his own G.I. Joe action figure! He was featured in several commercials for great companies like Coca Cola and McDonalds, and he was on almost every talk show across America. But after reaching his finish line, William Perry spiraled downwards into alcoholism.

So, how do you avoid the end-game illusion? How do you keep going even when it seems you have reached the peak of your achievements? Here's how.

The Journey is the Destination

Begin to shift your perception to see the journey to your goal as the destination. Okay, I know that may be tricky for some people to wrap their heads around so I'm going to say it differently.

Look forward to the process of getting to the success and not the success itself. In other words, the steps required to reach your goal should be more important than the goal itself. Remember, it is the process that actually makes you who you need to become before you attain your goal. So focus on the process and not just the end result.

For example, if you have a goal of losing weight, keep your focus on going to the gym or the process of working out rather than the 30 pounds you are trying to shed off. If your goal is to become a bestselling author and sell 10 million copies of your book, fix your attention on improving your writing skills and write consistently. That way, when you eventually reach your goal of losing the weight or sell the desired number of copies, you won't start spiraling downwards because there are no more heights to aspire to.

So, go ahead and:

- Create goals but don't take your eyes off the process of reaching them. Enjoy the journey because that is the destination you seek.

- Celebrate the attainment of milestones and use them as springboards for launching into greater heights.

- Create new goals even if they don't relate to your previous goals. Greater height doesn't necessarily mean breaking a previous record; however, it means remaining relevant in your field and even branching out to make giant strides in other areas.

- Aim for progress, not a particular outcome. Be open to whatever way progress will lead you instead of limiting yourself to some societal expectation of success.

In the next chapter, we'll take a look at why you hit plateaus and how to get out of them. But before then, understand that success plateaus are not necessarily a bad thing. See them as brief moments where you catch your breath along your journey to the top of the mountain. Plateaus become a bad thing when you convert them to permanent places of abode.

Chapter 7: Getting Out Of Success

Plateaus

"Growth comes at the point of resistance. We learn by pushing ourselves and finding what really lies at the outer reaches of our abilities." (Josh Waitzkin; Author, American Chess Player, Martial Arts Competitor)

Okay, so why do we hit plateaus? Here are some of the reasons and what you can do to get yourself out of them as quickly as possible.

Aiming for Perfection

You are never going to attain perfection no matter how hard you try. Using perfection as a driving force that motivates you to perform better is a good thing, but the question is: how many people who are focused on perfection ever get started? And even when they do, how long does it take them to take steps forward due to analysis paralysis? Focusing on perfection tends to get people stuck. Don't fall for that trap!

Here's what you should do instead. Take baby steps towards your goals no matter how imperfect the steps may be. Imperfect forward movement is better than over analyzing and staying stuck.

Monotonous Routine

Once the activities involved in getting you towards your goals starts to feel like a monotonous routine, you are heading towards a plateau. When you use the same approach all of the time in your businesses, relationships, or in any aspect of your life, those aspects will gradually become immune to the once-amazing effect of that approach.

What you will want to do to avoid monotony and complacency is to introduce diversity in your approach. Take a different route, change the routine, shake things up a bit, rearrange your workspace or bedroom, change your techniques, ask for someone else's view on how to do things differently, do whatever you can to bring in freshness and stimulate new ideas. You need to modify or introduce changes so that you don't get bored even by success. "*If nothing changes, nothing changes. If you keep doing what you're doing, you're going to keep getting what you're getting. You want change, make some.*" (Courtney C. Stevens, *The Lies About Truth*, 2015.)

Avoiding Challenges

Of all the reasons why we build mansions to live in on plateaus instead of taking quick rests, avoiding challenges has a black belt! *"C'mon what's the point in raising the stakes? We're already making enough sales!"* and that's how you take your foot off the pedal and allow complacency to set in.

The individuals and corporations who are willing to go head to head with a challenge are usually the ones breaking the records, making steady progress, and not settling for the status quo. Okay, I said head to head. Strike that out if you don't like confrontations and replace it with toe to toe if that works for you. The point is you should face those challenges either head-on or toe-on!

Applying Short-Term Solutions to Long-Term Problems

This is another way of saying you're addicted to shortcuts even at your own detriment. Trying to apply short-term solutions, no matter how awesome they may be, to long-term problems without properly considering the long-term consequences of that solution is a perfect shortcut to success plateaus. The reason is simple: you are putting round pegs in square holes; it doesn't work.

To avoid this trap, look beyond the immediate gratification you may derive from any quick fixes. Always keep in mind that you are in for the long haul and not just for some immediate gains that don't last. No finish line, remember? So, there's no point in trying to take shortcuts to get to the end of something that has no end. When you try to reach an end, you set yourself up for complacency.

Wrong Timing

Right timing is everything when it comes to making your efforts count. Massive action timed wrongly will yield little to no result, making your efforts ineffective. It is not just how much effort you put in that matters but also when the effort is applied. When you blow past every milestone without pausing to catch your breath, you are heading straight for a success plateau that may take a long while to recover from.

To wriggle your way out of this type of plateau is a bit

tricky because you may be thinking that success plateaus are all about inactivity and complacency or rest. But that's not always the case. The key is to find a balance between action and rest. You'll crash and burn if you do not rest when it is time to rest.

It is like trying to continue a speech when the applause is very high; no one is hearing the words you are speaking because they are reveling in your previous words. Take a cue, pause, and wait for the applause to subside before continuing your speech.

Rest is very important for you to recover. If you do not rest you'll start retrogressing which is even worse than plateauing.

You need rest from work. Many insights and creative ideas come to you when you are not working.

You need rest from food. Give your body time to recover from digesting food and allow it to utilize the energy it has stored. You can't be in a state of balanced health and fitness if you continue eating without adequate rest.

You need rest from physical exercise. Your body requires time to recover from workouts, or else your efforts at building or maintain muscles will be wasted.

You need rest from the day. Sleep well. If you understand the opportunity presented in the sleep state, you will look forward to it the way new lovers yearn to see each other! Sleep gives you the opportunity to reprogram your subconscious mind which controls about 90 to 95% of your waking moments.

"The conscious two-thirds of our life on earth is measured by the degree of attention we give sleep. Our understanding of and delight in what sleep has to bestow will cause us, night after night, to set out for it as though we were keeping an appointment with a lover." (Neville Goddard, Feeling Is The Secret)

Important Note

There is a difference between a success plateau and a success terminal point. Sometimes, you may try all the tricks in all the books and they simply don't work. That's a strong sign that you may have reached a terminal point. Stop flogging a dead horse; do something else. Always remember what I pointed out in the previous chapter: greater height doesn't necessarily mean breaking your previous records in the same field. Switch to something that will advance you personally and professionally.

Chapter 8: Get Clear

"As you sow in your subconscious mind, so shall you reap in your body and environment." (Joseph Murphy, 1898 – 1981; Irish born New Thought Minister)

This is a chapter you wouldn't want to skip for anything! I'll keep it short and simple but don't be deceived by its simplicity. The key to success is clarity; that's probably no news. What's news, however, is how to get clear. I have presented below, simple steps that will help you clarify your vision. These steps go beyond the usual yarn of *"be specific about your goals so that it becomes clear."* We are taking a trip deep into your subconscious to rewrite the programs that are stopping you from getting clear.

Your Subconscious Mind and Your Goals

Your conscious mind is creative; it can formulate thoughts, ideas, and goals based on your wishes and desires. The problem with us humans is that we rarely focus on the present. We are either thinking of the future or the past. And in those moments when you are not paying attention to the present, you have turned over control of your life to your subconscious mind. This usually happens for more than 90% of your day.

Your subconscious mind is a set of programs that run on autopilot and continue to work 24/7 (just in case you don't know, that means, all day, every day). It is like a tape recorder playing back your experiences and trying to protect you from experiences that caused you pain in the past or experiences whose outcome is unknown to it.

So, while your goal may be formulated using your conscious mind, if they do not align with the program in your subconscious mind, the subconscious mind will do all in its power to sabotage the realization of that goal no matter how nice and dandy it is. This is usually the case with most of us since our subconscious programming is mostly negative.

What to do then? Rewrite the programs in your subconscious mind to align with your wishes and desires. That way, even when you are not focused consciously on your day to day activities, your subconscious, which runs your affairs for more than 90% of your day, is working in your favor.

This is not a bunch of New Age crap. No. It's pure science. Neuroscience has shown that the brain can be rewired and new neural pathways can be deliberately created to help us develop and retain new habits.

Here's how to rewrite your subconscious program. Please pay close attention here. If you get this right, you can be, do, and have anything you desire. Then the saying will be true in your life, *"whatever the mind of man can conceive and believe it can achieve."* (Napoleon Hill, 1883 – 1970; American Self-Help Author)

Do This Daily

At Night

Every night before you go to sleep, give your subconscious something to work on. *"Never go to sleep without a request to your subconscious."* (Thomas Edison, 1847 – 1931; American Inventor and Businessman)

Here's how to do that:

- An hour before bedtime, unplug from your gadgets and screens (TV, phone, tablet, laptop, or computer – too many screens these days!) Don't check your emails or social media updates. Reconnect with yourself (if you are alone) or with your family and loved ones. Rest from the day's activities so that you can recover physically and mentally.

- Just before you sleep, take about 5 to 10 minutes to really think about what you would like to accomplish the next day or what problem(s) you would like to solve or find a solution to.

- Place your alarm across the room away from your bed so that you must get up and walk across the room to turn it off in the morning.

- Go to bed and sleep for at least 7 hours. I know this may be asking too much for some people, but if your body must fully recover, you need to get adequate and quality sleep. As you sleep, your subconscious takes your order (the goals or problems you thought about) and begins to work on them to create neural pathways in your brain to help you identify ways to meet your target in your waking moments.

"The conditions and events of your life are your children formed from the molds of your subconscious impressions in sleep. They are made in the image and likeness of your innermost feeling that they may reveal you to yourself." (Neville Goddard, *Feeling Is The Secret*)

In the Morning

When you wake up in the morning:

- Don't reach for your smartphone! Unless your alarm is set on your smartphone. Cultivate the habit of keeping your smartphone out of your bedroom.

- Spend 5 to 15 minutes in meditation or prayer.

- Spend another 20 – 30 minutes writing down insights in your journal. Please use a pen or pencil and write with your hand (like humans do in time past!) Don't type your insights or goals on your tablet, laptop, or phone. Don't plug in or connect to your gadgets and electronics just yet. Journaling stimulates the flow of ideas from your subconscious mind in the form of insights and creative ideas.

- Write down your goals for the day in your journal even if you don't have any insights or aha moments. As you put down your goals, you are reinforcing the new programs for your subconscious mind.

- Connect with your family. Do some physical exercise. Have a cold shower. And go on with your day.

Bottom Line

When you wake up in the morning and begin to immediately worry about the problems of the previous day, or you instinctively reach for your smartphone, it is a sign that you are living from a place of reaction. You are not living your life by design but by reacting to what others have set out for you. I once saw a meme from the Spirit Science website that beautifully captures the addictive nature of phones. It says, "*I finally realized it. People are prisoners of the phones, that's why they are called cell phones!*"

Rushing into your day doesn't necessarily guarantee more productivity or more success. Many people rush into their day out of habit or a need to be at some place at a specific time. This is far removed from a need to be more productive or successful. Deliberately slowing down at the start of each day and connecting to the essence of who you really are, and then focusing on the steps you need to take to achieve your goals for that day will ultimately lead to more productivity and more success.

When you form the habit of deliberately rewriting the programs in your subconscious mind, you take back control of your life and you are no longer being rushed into your day. Your mind is clear as to what you want to achieve and you are heading straight for it. The practice I have described above may appear simple, but the results are profound and life-altering (in a good way, so don't be alarmed!). It will help you to maximize the use of your time to focus on things that help you reach your goals and solve problems instead of wasting a large chunk of your day in unproductive ventures.

Getting clear requires that you unburden your mind from distractions, especially self-inflicted and addictive distractions. If you must achieve goals that are beyond your reach, you must be in the driver's seat of your life. I am not suggesting that you throw away your gadgets; I am simply advocating a proper, controlled, and mindful use of them realizing that they can easily steal away a precious resource – time – which can never be regained.

"One look at an email can rob you of 15 minutes of focus. One call on your cell phone, one tweet, one instant message can destroy your schedule, forcing you to move meetings, or blow off really important things, like love, and friendship." (Jacqueline Leo, Editor)

Chapter 9: Can You See Your Goals?

"To be realized, then, the wish must be resolved into the feeling of being or having or witnessing the state sought. This is accomplished by assuming the feeling of the wish fulfilled." (Neville Goddard, 1905 – 1972; Author and Teacher)

You are not what you want to be is simply because you cannot see yourself being that which you want. You cannot be, do, or have what you cannot visualize yourself being, doing, or having. Bob Proctor, an American author, motivational speaker, and a success coach puts it succinctly when he said, *"Thoughts become things. If you see it in your mind, you will hold it in your hand."*

Remember, in the previous chapter, we talked about assigning your subconscious mind with tasks to perform while you drift off to sleep. If you go to sleep feeling worried, depressed, unfulfilled, and generally in a negative frame of mind, well guess what? Your subconscious takes that as a directive to work on and it will faithfully deliver more of such in your waking moments. You will self-sabotage all your efforts towards reaching your goals because you can't see them accomplished. All you see are obstacles, reasons why you can't make it.

As Neville puts it, *"The feeling which comes in response to the question, 'How would I feel were my wish realized?' is the feeling which should monopolize and immobilize your attention as you relax into sleep. You must be in the consciousness of being or having that which you want to be or to have before you drop off to sleep."*

But I am not suggesting that if you merely close your eyes and see your goals accomplished they will magically be accomplished without you lifting a finger! That is as ridiculous as it is incorrect.

Here's what I mean by clearly seeing and visualizing your goals. Sit down and write out what it is you want to accomplish (and please don't close your eyes while writing!). Breakdown what you have written into short-term goals (daily and weekly goals), medium-term goals (3 month goals or thereabout), and long-term goals (a year and above). Now, begin to feel as if your short-term goals are already accomplished. Forget the medium and long-term goals for now, just concentrate on the short-term goals.

Visualization without a corresponding feeling is like shooting blanks; you're not going to get any meaningful results with that. See yourself having accomplished your daily goals and it will open you up to insights, creative ideas, and the motivation to take inspired action towards its fulfillment.

Take It One Step At A Time

Resist the temptation to set too many goals for your day. Motivation has the tendency to make you feel like you can take on the entire world all by yourself and all at once! But after a while, you'll realize you have bitten off more than you can chew and then you start to gradually omit some of your daily goals. This has a negative psychological impact on you, as you will begin to see yourself as being unable to stick to your commitments.

In order to avoid this trap, start with very few daily goals. You can begin with just one goal as long as it is something that will make you feel fulfilled at the end of the day. Then, when you have mastered how to overcome inertia and procrastination, you can gradually increase your daily goals. One goal a day may seem too little, but imagine what your life will be like if you can achieve just one goal per day for a whole year. That's 365 different goals in just one year! (366 goals in a leap year.)

Moreover, whatever goals you set have to be concrete goals. Concrete goals are time-bound, specific, and measurable.

Here's a slight addition to the evening routine we discussed in the previous chapter. To increase the speed with which you are able to accomplish your goals, see and feel your daily goals as if they were already accomplished as you drift off to sleep.

"Sleep is the door into heaven. What you take in as a feeling you bring out as a condition, action, or object in space. So sleep in the feeling of the wish fulfilled." (Neville Goddard)

Do This

Aside from visualizing and feeling the feelings of accomplishment, you need to take action. And by action, I don't mean rushing into your day and multitasking. That's not it at all. To see your goals clearly, ask yourself:

1. What do I want to do? Write it down. (See and feel it in your mind at night, and then write it in your journal in the morning.)

2. When do I want to do it? Write down the exact time you want to start working on your daily goal.

3. How do I want to do it? Write down the steps you need to take to reach your goal for that day.

So, if you were thinking this was another *"lie down, close your eyes, feel good, and your goals will manifest,"* theory, well, sorry to burst your bubble. It doesn't work that way!

Chapter 10: Do You Believe In Your Goals?

"Believe in yourself! Have faith in your abilities! Without a humble but reasonable confidence in your own powers, you cannot be successful or happy." (Norman Vincent Peale, 1898 - 1993; Minister and Author)

Bring out your goal book. Go ahead, don't be shy. Just do it. (*PS. no one is watching!*) Now that you have your book in hand, go through it and see that goal or those goals that you always skip over. The time always just doesn't seem right for them yet. You'll do them later, only that you never actually get to do them. And even if you don't have a goal book (get one!) mentally call up your goals and see the ones you always procrastinate.

Do you know why it is easy to procrastinate or skip them? Because you never really believe in them, period!

And why don't you believe in those goals? Because there is a fundamental error in the way you see yourself. You have a false premise that you are deficient in some ways, so you probably are not going to be able to achieve those goals even if you attempt to. The easiest way out is to simply skip them for the time being. You'll get to them when you must have acquired sufficient capability to take on the goals. Problem is: you never get to acquire the capability.

The truth is you are not deficient in any way! You may need to work on yourself to improve your capability, but you never really are in any form of deficiency to achieve any of your desires. The desire in you to achieve the goal is a sure indication that you have the capability to attain it. "*All there is of possibility is seeking expression through men... God, the One Substance, is trying to live and do and enjoy things through humanity... If you fix upon your consciousness the fact that the desire you feel for the possession of riches is one with the desire of Omnipotence for more complete expression, your faith becomes invincible.*" (Wallace D. Wattles, *The Science Of Getting Rich*)

Do This

1. Grab a pen and paper. Don't start writing yet. Simply and honestly ask yourself, "*What is stopping me from believing in my ability to achieve this goal?*" Reflect on that for a moment.

2. Now put down the reasons you think are stopping you. Be down-to-earth about this. Don't sugar coat it, don't try to make it your fault. Write it the way you see it. If it is a challenge you think is beyond you, write it. If

it is due to your unserious attitude, write it. Whatever it is, just write it down. Remember, no one is watching but you.

3. Now take a moment to read through what you have written and begin to seek solutions to the seemingly insurmountable challenges as well as ways to improve your unserious attitude (if that is the case).

Take all the time you need to work on this exercise. If your mind is not coming up with any feasible solutions, let it be for now. But when you go to bed today (not tomorrow or some other time; today!) fixate upon how to come up with the solutions you seek and drift off to sleep in that state of mind. Allow your subconscious mind to work its magic!

If you really want to stop procrastinating the attainment of your goals, then stop taking the easy way out. The easy way out is listening to enticing distractions that offer you temporal satisfaction as long as it will keep your mind off your glaring unwillingness to take on the challenge of working towards your goals. To make matters worse, these distractions are mostly thieves of your valuable time. They make your day slip by and you go to bed feeling less about yourself; believing you are a failure and incapable of attaining success.

Say no to distractions. Keep digging until you find a solution to that which is stopping you from having 100% confidence in yourself. You must have a deep conviction about who you are and what you are capable of before you can stretch yourself beyond your normal reach.

"The future belongs to those who believe in the beauty of their dreams." (Eleanor Roosevelt, 1884 – 1962; First Lady of the United States from 1933 to 1945)

Chapter 11: Achieve Your Goals

"Do not wait; the time will never be 'just right.'
Start where you stand, and work with whatever
tools you may have at your command, and
better tools will be found as you go along."
(George Herbert, 1593 – 1633; Poet, Orator, and
Priest)

Seeing and feeling your goals as well as believing that
you can achieve them will all amount to zero, nada,
utter waste of time, energy, and effort if you fail to
take physical actions that will result in the attainment
of your goals.

We live in a physical world; and just in case you don't
know, it is called planet earth. For things to be
actualized here on this physical planet, you need to
take physical action. Visualizing and believing are all
good and necessary, but they won't do the pushups
and sit-ups, eat healthily, do the research, put in
more hours at work, improve your work ethic, climb
the tallest mountain, deliver speeches and
presentations publicly, or whatever it is your personal
and professional goals are. They certainly won't dig
up gold, purify them, and then send them tumbling
into your treasure box! Metaphysical or spiritual
processes do not magically manifest your goals in a
physical world without some form of physical activity.
As Mr. Wattles puts it, *"By thought, you can cause*

the gold in the hearts of the mountains to be impelled toward you; but it will not mine itself, refine itself, coin itself into double eagles, and come rolling along the roads seeking its way into your pocket." (Wallace D. Wattles, *The Science of Getting Rich, 1910*)

To achieve your goals, you need to set aside time on a daily basis to physically work on them. It is not necessary to do all the things you need to do in one giant step; do the little things that all contribute to the attainment of your goals. In other words, anything that can draw you closer to your goal is what you should be spending time on.

Here are the fundamentals you will need in order to achieve your goals (especially the big, long-term goals):

1. The mindset;

2. The necessary skills; and

3. The tools.

We have covered mindset in chapters 9 and 10. When you can see, feel, and believe in your goals and dreams, then you have the right mindset.

Now, you need to acquire the right skills for the attainment of your goals. You need to invest in the knowledge that will build your skills. As an example, if your goal is to write a best-selling book, do you have the skills – the capacity to do that? How well do you know how to write? How well do you practice writing? How much have you invested in yourself to improve your knowledge in writing? If you are scared of investing in yourself to develop the necessary skills, then I'm afraid there's something wrong with your self-confidence. You'll need to still work on your mindset.

The tools you need are in the form of capital, the right technology, equipment, and other resources that are relevant to help you attain your goals. For example, if one of your goals is to lose weight, you cannot effectively do that without having enough money to provide you with a healthy diet. If building muscle is one of your goals, you cannot possibly do that without having the right workout tools (or improvised ones). Your writing goal may meet a dead end without the right tools like money to invest in a writing course, a computer or laptop, money to purchase the right software and editing tools, etc. Do you get the gist? Good.

Take Action

Knowing what to do and how to do it is one thing; doing it is another. So, let's see how you can take practical steps towards achieving your goals.

1. Invest in yourself. The scarier the investment the better, because somewhere in the recess of

your mind, a thought along the lines of, "*I can't let such huge investment go to waste*" will make you stay committed to making the investment count. People usually don't value what they don't pay for, right? Moreover, taking action that involves monetary commitment sends a powerful message to your mind that you are indeed ready. Action is a self-signaling activity.

2. Set a time frame for achieving the goal. Without a sense of urgency, you probably won't achieve anything significant, especially in a world full of distractions. Time-bound goals are more likely to be achieved. Time frame enables you to measure your progress.

3. Set a negative consequence if you didn't achieve your goal within the time frame. For example, give up all social media interactions for a whole month or donate $1,000 to a course you absolutely detest if you don't reach your goal on or before the deadline. Let the consequence be something you would never want to do. This will compel you to tap into your creativity and resourcefulness.

4. Designate specific times on a daily basis dedicated to that goal. You need to schedule your daily activities to accommodate the achievement of your goal. Decide on the amount of time you will allocate daily to your goal and ensure that you stay true to the

schedule.

5. Avoid all forms of distractions. Screens seem to be a major source of distraction in our world today. Phone screens, TV screens, laptops, computers, and tablets are constantly trying to get a piece of us. Unless your goal requires you to work with screens, keep them far away from you especially when it is time to work on your goals. Other distractions like family, friends, work colleagues, study mates, etc. can be controlled by letting them know you are working on achieving your goals and will require some privacy or alone time (unless your goal requires working with one or more people).

6. Make your goals public. Here's a good use of your social media account: announce your decision on all your social media platforms. This is one good way to burn your ship, blow the bridge, and hit a point of no return! You must deliver or else face public embarrassment. Before you begin to protest, I know that not all goals are meant for public consumption (especially if you have identified yourself as a rebel who is not motivated by external accountability), so chill out. No one can force you to make something you deem very personal a topic for public consumption. I'll bet my left kidney you're smiling now, right? Here's the catch. You must find a way to be more committed to strictly personal goals

or else you will always fall flat on your face each time you attempt to reach those goals. Why? No one is watching, so the stakes aren't high enough.

7. Be accountable to someone unbiased. Have you ever wondered why people in a board meeting appear cold and without feeling? It's because they don't care about whatever justifications others have about not meeting a specific target. All they are simply interested in is the result. Find someone who is not emotionally invested in you to hold you accountable. This will make you forget about your excuses and focus on producing results, especially if the person is an authority figure.

Chapter 12: Total Commitment

"There's a difference between interest and commitment. When you're interested in doing something, you do it only when circumstance permit. When you're committed to something, you accept no excuses, only results." (Art Turock, Motivational Business Speaker)

Ah, well, you win some, you lose some. That's just life! Really? That sounds to me like the self-talk of someone who is not 100% committed to pursuing their dreams. It sounds to me like someone who says they want something but deep within them they are not willing to do whatever it takes to achieve that something. How badly do you really want to lose that excess weight you carry around? How soon do you want to bid farewell to the famous, *"I can't afford it"* line? Are you really ready to improve your work ethic and earn that promotion? How soon would you like to become an expert in your field? Do you still want to have your name boldly printed on the cover page of the #1 selling book of the year?

Or should we just shelve some of your goals and leave them on the backburner and concentrate on a few convenient ones? After all, *you win some, you lose some. That's just life*, eh?

What is common with the following words: suicide,

pesticide, genocide, homicide, and biocide? They all end with the suffix "cide" which means to kill or killing. The word "***decide***" happens to fall into the "kill" category also. Once you make up your mind to pursue a dream, to achieve a goal, and to aspire to something higher, you must first decide to be committed to that dream, goal, or aspiration. In other words, you must first de-cide (kill every other option) and be left with only one option – the achievement of your goal.

If your goals are "*nice to have,*" but not "*need to have,*" then you can play around without being really committed to them. If you have not burnt your ship of excuses, you are not yet ready to make a 100% commitment to your dreams, goals, and aspirations. "*Anyone can dabble, but once you've made that commitment, your blood has that particular thing in it, and it's very hard for people to stop you.*" (Bill Cosby; American Stand-up Comedian, Author, Actor, and Musician)

Kill Off Unhelpful Relationships

One of the things that can drag you back and keep you held up in your old ways is unhelpful relationships. You need to examine your relationships with the people you spend a lot of time with and determine if your interactions are pushing you towards your goals or keeping you away from achieving your goals. But wait! Don't rush into making enemies out of the people in your life. That's very far from what I am suggesting. As a matter of fact, they are not responsible for whatever stagnation you have experienced in your life. So, it's not their fault, and neither is it yours either. It is the fault of your limiting beliefs. Thankfully, you can change them if you want.

To determine which relationship is helpful to you, do this exercise.

1. Make 2 lists. On the first list, write down the top 10 things you want to achieve in the next week.

2. On the second list, write down the people you interacted with physically, by email, phone call, text, social media, etc., for the entire week. Obviously, this will have to be done daily, most probably at night.

3. Assign a value from 0 to 10 to the name of each person on the second list. The value should represent the level to which that person helped you in some way towards reaching your goals with 0 being absolutely no help and 10 being the highest level of help.

At first, this exercise will leave you shocked at the number of unproductive interactions you have on a daily basis. And then, you will begin to be deliberate about your time and who you spend it with. But don't go hating people – that, apparently, is not my intention.

Chapter 13: Stop Arguing For Your Limitations

"Argue for your limitations, and sure enough they're yours." (Richard Bach, American Writer)

If you really want to reach your goals, then you have to give up the excuses you make for your limitations. Until you are fed up and decide to let go of the things that are holding you back from reaching your goals, you will not be able to take your goals off the pages of a book and make them into your reality.

You see, there is hardly anybody that isn't committed to something. The question is: to what are you committed? Where does your loyalty lie? To your excuses (limitations) or to the ideas and ideals that are constantly beckoning on you to rise beyond your current level? Are you committed to harmful choices and detrimental behaviors? Are you addicted to distractions from your environment? You have to be brutally honest with yourself in answering these questions if success and progress in all areas of your life mean anything to you.

I find the story of a man who climbed up to the summit of Mount Everest really inspiring. In 2006, Mark Inglis, from New Zealand, made his way steadily up to the top of the highest mountain on planet earth. But there's nothing too spectacular about climbing a mountain, or is there? Well, there's actually nothing too awe-inspiring about it, unless the climber has no legs!

Mark Inglis had both legs amputated in 1982 following an intense blizzard that had him and his partner trapped on the top of Mount Cook for 13 days. He and his partner's legs were damaged by frost while they were waiting for rescue. Being a double amputee seemed like a powerful limitation to stop anyone from even the most basic use of the legs which is walking. Not Inglis! He went back to Mount Cook and climbed up to its summit in January of 2002. And as if that wasn't enough, in 2004 he went on to be the only second double amputee to climb up the Cho Oyu Mountain which was greater than 26,000 ft (8,000 meters) in height.

He became the first ever double amputee to climb up to the summit of Mount Everest. It wasn't a smooth climb. Inglis fell from a height of 21,000 ft (6,400 meters) while acclimatizing and he broke one of his prosthetic legs. Was that enough to stop Inglis? He refused to argue for his limitations and eventually made it to the top of Mount Everest in spite of all the physical limitations.

Whenever I see a picture of Nick Vujicic, it reminds me to not give in to any of my excuses; zero limitations is my watchword. Wait, what? You mean you have not heard of Nick? He was born without arms and legs, lived utterly hopeless, contemplated suicide by drowning at age 10, shifted his focus from his glaring limitations, and went on to become a world-renowned motivational speaker, husband, father of 4, and a very wealthy evangelist. He truly has no arms, no legs, and certainly no excuses!

But this chapter is not about Mark Inglis or Nick Vujicic. It is about you and the attainment of your goals. What, again, are your excuses? What are those things you believe are stopping you from being, doing, and having the things that are important to you?

Here's a list of common limitations:

1. I'm neck deep in debt.

2. I don't have money.

3. I don't have the required experience.

4. My health and fitness isn't at par.

5. Someone is against my progress.

6. My partner is not supportive.

7. I come from a poor background.

8. My childhood was very difficult.

9. I am handicapped.

10. I was raped/abused.

11. I was a victim of a disaster.

12. The government is insensitive to our plight (this excuse will probably win the contest if you were looking for the most common excuse used throughout the world!).

13. The economy is not stable.

14. I am too old for that.

15. I am too young for that.

16. These things are beyond my control.

17. I don't know influential people / I don't have the right connections.

18. My life hasn't been easy.

19. Luck is just not on my side.

Oh, if your limitation is not on this list, please do add it.

Remember that if you continue to see yourself as incapable of anything, you are programming your subconscious with that belief, and you are most definitely going to get more of such incapabilities showing up in every area of your life.

In other words:

- Your health and fitness will not improve if your focus is on why you can't eat healthily or workout. For example, I don't have the money to register for gym sessions. Following a diet program is too difficult for me. I don't have time to cook my own food.

- Your relationship with your significant other cannot improve if you keep focusing on your shortcomings in the relationship. For example, I am not a good lover. I am not good at communicating my feelings. I have failed in my past relationships and this current one may not be an exception. My parents are divorced that's why I can't keep a relationship.

- You will not double your income if your attention is on all the reasons why you can't. For example, my job takes all my time, I can't find extra hours to take on a second job. I am afraid of losing my investment if I give my money to some stranger to manage my investments. Most passive income streams are highly risky to invest in.

- You will never get through school or get the grades you know you can if you keep thinking, *"my kids are taking all my time."* *"I am too old for this."* *"I hate this course."*

Your circumstances and environment are simply a reflection of your beliefs. *As A Man Thinketh* by James Allen is both the title of his book and a verse in the Bible that says you are what you think in your heart. This means you are exactly at a place in your life that you believe you should be right now whether that place is pleasant or not. Whatever is your life's situation right now is exactly what you want. If you truly don't want it, then you would have had what it is you preferred.

So, if where you are right now in relation to your goals is very unpleasing to you, begin right at this moment to change your beliefs about what you can and cannot do. Stop allowing external circumstances (which you created by the way) limit you.

If it is a skill you need to learn, by all means, start immediately.

If you need to drop some habits, go ahead and drop them.

If you need to cut off some relationships, by God do it!

Until you are willing to let go of your limitations, you are not going to make much progress towards achieving your goals.

Chapter 14: Getting Versus Giving

– The Secret To Success

"Giving is the master key to success, in all applications of human life." (Bryant McGill; Author, Activist, and Social Entrepreneur)

A child can drive its parents out of their skin just to get him or her a toy. Once they get the toy, the joy and excitement wanes; they will soon forget about playing with the toy they so eagerly wanted. This is so because they are children and never really take the time to think about why they want what they want.

Adults, on the other hand, should ideally know why they want what they want, right? But do they? Do you?

"What's in it for me?"

That's the primary motivation for most people. If your focus is only on the benefits that can be derived from attaining success, once you get the benefits, the motivation goes out the window and you will no longer be interested in pursuing further progress.

This brings us back to where we began this book: what is your "why?" A superficial "why" is fleeting; that is the more reason you should dig deep to find a far-reaching purpose to anchor your actions.

The reason why you want to achieve goals beyond your reach must be based on your intense desire to share or give and not just to get.

Here's what I'll recommend that you do right now. Go to a quiet place, perhaps under a tree, and chew on a piece of straw, then ask yourself, am I focused on giving or getting?

- Why do you want to double or 10x your income? Is it to have your face on the cover of a magazine or to be able to fully express love and care for yourself and others around you?

- Why do you want a sexy body, and why do you want to develop abs? Why do you want to lose weight? Is it solely for the accolades or to be a shining example to others of what is humanly possible? Is it for the attention you'll get when you walk into a room or for the person you will become in the process? Is it for the purpose of fitting into sexy dresses or for the purpose of teaching others how to eat healthily and live a healthy lifestyle?

- Why do you want to be a bestselling author? Is it because of the fame and fortune or because you want people to really learn from the messages in your book? Is it to give your resume a facelift or to transform your readers' lives?

- Why do you seek that job promotion? Is it so that you can sit at the head of the table during meetings or is it because you want a position that calls forth more of what is deposited in you? Are you seeking to impress your colleagues or to positively impact the workplace?

- Why are you trying to break a previous record? Are you doing it basically for the fame or are you focused on raising the bar so that others behind will have to stretch themselves further before reaching and eventually crossing the bar?

- Why do you want to be closer to your significant other? Is it to get more attention from them or to give them your all? Is it to get more affection and care from them or to share your love and affection with them?

"By becoming the answer to someone's prayer, we often find the answers to our own." (Dieter F. Uchtdorf; German Aviator and Religious Leader)

You see, the thing about receiving is that you cannot sustain it without giving. Take love as an example, it cannot be experienced without giving it out. You have to be loving and lovable before you can experience love from another person.

"If you go looking for a friend, you're going to find they're scarce. If you go out to be a friend, you'll find them everywhere." (Zig Ziglar, 1926 – 2012; American Author, Salesperson, and Motivational Speaker)

In other words, you need to become the person who does what you are seeking before you can have or get what you are seeking. This is the true definition of the "be, do, have" process.

So while you are still contemplating under the tree or whatever quiet place you choose to sit in, and gently chewing on your straw, do all you can to tie your goals to a purpose that is beyond mere compensation, remuneration, personal gains, and base motives. Aim for a purpose that is higher than you. You may not have a purpose like banishing hunger from planet earth or something dramatic, but you definitely can think of something that doesn't start and end with only you.

Remember that if your focus is purely on what's in it for you, you will most likely abandon the quest for improvement once you get "what's in it for you." It is the pursuit of something higher than you that keeps you in the continual quest for improvement, refinement, and advancement of your desires long after you have gotten "what's in it for you!"

Always remember this powerful line from one time British Prime Minister: *"We make a living by what we get. We make a life by what we give."* (Winston S. Churchill, 1874 – 1965; Prime Minister of the United Kingdom from 1940 to 1945)

Chapter 15: Selflessness Leads To

Success

"Don't aim at success. The more you aim at it and make it a target, the more you are going to miss it. For success, like happiness, cannot be pursued; it must ensue, and it only does so as the unintended side effect of one's personal dedication to a cause greater than oneself or as the by-product of one's surrender to a person other than oneself. " (Viktor E. Frankl, 1905 – 1997; Australian Neurologist and Psychiatrist)

But what is wrong with doing something for the purpose of compensation? Nothing! There's absolutely nothing wrong in seeking some form of compensation for whatever it is you are doing. However, when compensation is the only driving force behind what you are doing, then your success is limited or directly proportional to the compensation you receive.

For example, if you get paid $100 for putting in 5 hours of work per day, then as soon as the time clocks 5 hours, you will put down all tools and demand for your pay.

The faulty line of question and reasoning for someone

who is solely focused on short-term success goes something like this:

- Why should I keep working longer than 5 hours when no one is going to pay me for the extra time?

- Why should I continue writing new books when I have already attained the status of a bestselling author?

- Why should I work harder when I have already earned the promotion?

- What's the point in learning new ways to entice, seduce, and show affection to my spouse when we are already married?

Do you now see how shallow self-gratifying reasons will truncate new heights of achievements? For you to surpass mundane success and stretch yourself to reach for goals that seem beyond your reach, you need to become selfless about achieving success.

When you are obsessed with success, it will elude you. The reason is simple: obsession means to focus on yourself. Once you get what you are obsessed with, the desire for it is satisfied and there will be no motivation to improve upon the success.

Selflessness leads you to:

- Discover new ways to do something that wouldn't have been possible if you were focused only on self-gratification.

- Easily overcome success plateaus and keep moving in the direction of your ideals.

- Give more of yourself to others even when it appears that you are depleted.

- Go the extra mile, which, by the way, is less crowded, and then achieve true success!

Selflessness makes you find your true self! But this cannot make any sense to you if you still hold the false premise that setting and achieving goals is solely for the purpose of acquiring and accumulating things that are meant for us alone. *"The best way to find yourself is to lose yourself in the service of others."* (Mahatma Gandhi, 1869 – 1948; Indian Activist)

Realize that true success is a byproduct of what you genuinely do for a higher purpose. (Please read that again, slowly!)

So, develop the habit of losing yourself in the pursuit of your goals – do it as if there is no end in sight, because, truly, there is no finish line. Then, and only then, can your efforts result in true success, happiness, and personal development. Keep in mind that *"A candle loses nothing by lighting another candle."* (James Keller, 1900 – 1977; Clergyman)

Famous Selfless People

Bill Gates, Warren Buffett, Richard Branson, Gordon Moore, Jon Huntsman Sr., and Chuck Feeney are just a few names that are known for being selfless and hugely successful. But before you go screaming from the rooftop that these people are all billionaires, here is another list of selfless human beings who became highly successful and famous without seeking fame and fortune. (And I am not suggesting that being selfless means being poor or not wanting money – that is not the meaning of selflessness.)

1. Mahatma Gandhi (born Mohandas Karamchand Gandhi) didn't seek success for himself – he "fought" for his people and succeeded without so much as lifting a finger.

2. Mother Teresa (born Agnes Gonxha Bojaxhiu) had a goal to provide food for the needy. Without personally having millions or billions, she selflessly pursued her goal, constantly refining her ideals, and went from feeding a few needy individuals to people across 30 different countries of the world.

3. Martin Luther King, Jr. had a dream that was greater than his personal ambitions. Former President Barack Obama of the United States of America was the personification of that dream.

4. Paul Newman enjoyed a successful career as a Hollywood actor but wanted more than just the glitz and glamour. He co-founded

Newman's Own food products in 1982 and donated well over $250 million to charities from the profits generated. Before his death, children with incurable diseases had the benefit of experiencing outdoor activities in his 11 Hole-in-the-Wall camps worldwide.

"Eh, these are all dead people!" Wait, what? Is that even an excuse? First, billionaires, and now dead people? Okay, let's see a few individuals who are neither billionaires nor dead (at least the last time I checked!) and they are not the typical famous people either. They are your typical everyday people – just like you. Perhaps that will convince you to live a life of service to humanity; to convert your goals to ideals that are far beyond personal gains.

Shining Examples of Ordinary Selfless People

1. Anwar Khokhar: Cutting hair for a living doesn't typically make you rich and famous. But that doesn't stop Anwar Khokhar from living his selfless dream of reuniting lost and kidnapped children with their parents and guardians. Sources have put the number of children reunited between 8,500 and 11,000.

He doesn't get paid for this either. His source of livelihood is barbing, yet he finds true success from stretching himself beyond the struggle for daily survival ("Barber who has reunited," 2010).

2. Officer Damon Cole: This police officer, with the Forth Worth Police Department in Texas, takes it upon himself to travel hundreds of miles just to visit critically ill children while dressed in their favorite superhero costume. Talk about a real-life superhero! He lifts the spirits of children with failing health as he goes far and wide posing as Batman, Superman, Spiderman, Incredible Hulk, etc. He also travels long distances to attend kids' funerals in costumes that honor the memory of the child. His goal is definitely not motivated by personal gains but by selfless service to children (Stump, 2016).

3. Tejinder Singh: A man who repairs air conditioners by day and juggles that with cab driving at night, Tejinder Singh from Punjab, India, still finds the time and resources to cook meals on the last Sunday of every month to feed the homeless and hungry in Darwin, Australia. According to him, *"I do something for homeless people, so they get more energy so they're happy. My religion says 10% of income goes toward needy and poor people – no matter (whether) they belong to your religion or any religion"* ("Sikh Cab Driver,"

2015).

4. Saber Hosseini: Saber is a school teacher in Afghanistan who has come to be known as the founder of the mobile library in Afghanistan. His goal was not to be a world-renown teacher who makes the headline but that was the unavoidable result of selflessly pursuing his goal. And this is his goal: to increase literacy among children who live in parts of Afghanistan which are difficult to access due to bad terrain. He began doing this alone using a bike to transport hundreds of books since he couldn't get funding and the terrain wasn't particularly favorable for cars. Soon, volunteers joined him and a foundation called The Kids Foundation was established with about 20 volunteers who have delivered more than 6,000 books on bikes. This man has gradually shifted the negative perception about bikes which are used for terrorist bombings in Afghanistan to something very positive. Hosseini said, *"One time, I talked to children in a village about guns, using the slogan 'say no to guns and yes to books.' The next time I went to their village, the kids had gathered up all of their plastic toy guns and handed them over to me – but they had one condition: they wanted their village to be the first in the next round of book deliveries so that they could get first pick. It was the most joyful moment of my life!"* ("The cyclist

bringing," 2016).

5. Dr. Jim Withers: Risking his life in the quest to provide healthcare for people in the lowest echelons of society, Dr. Jim Withers was driven by a higher purpose to offer free medical services to sick people living in the most sinister and grimiest parts of Pittsburgh who couldn't afford it. Soon enough, other volunteers, doctors, nurses, and social workers joined Withers and his campaign grew into what is now known as Operation Safety Net which has so far treated about 10,000 street people, 1,200 of which the team had assisted in finding good housing (Melada, 2011).

I can easily fill this book with names of people who were selflessly successful and still not exhaust the list! But the list won't be incomplete because it is too long – no! The list is and will remain incomplete until it has your name added to it! You do not have to change the entire world, your country, or even your community before your name can be added to the list. Start from where you are and tailor your goals to positively affect at least one other person aside from yourself.

"Helping one person might not change the world, but it could change the world for one person." (Anonymous)

Chapter 16: Embrace Challenges

"The ultimate measure of a man is not where he stands in moments of comfort and convenience, but where he stands at times of challenge and controversy." (Martin Luther King, Jr., 1929 – 1968; American Baptist Minister and Activist)

What is the point of having an intelligent brain designed to solve problems and not have any problems to solve? Each of us is endowed with some type of innate ability to bring about progress in some aspect of human experience. What would be the purpose of that innate ability if everything were already perfect? What would be the point of living if there were no challenges to call forth growth from us?

I love how Wallace D. Wattles puts it in his book *The Science Of Getting Rich*, *"Every living thing must continually seek for the enlargement of its life, because life, in the mere act of living, must increase itself."*

I bet you, your life will be a complete bore if you run away from challenges. Whether you call it challenges or problems doesn't really matter, what matters is, if you are not in the habit of continually stretching yourself beyond your current station in life, you are gradually dying; because to live is to increase.

And here's the crux of the matter: you cannot continually seek to solve problems or challenges if your focus is on self-gratification. You must aim for a goal beyond the ego-self. You must aspire for things that benefit not just you, but everyone involved. If you include others in your quest for attaining your goals, you lift the bar beyond mere selfish reasons and in the process, you will achieve more than you have ever imagined.

"You will get all you want in life, if you help enough other people get what they want." (Zig Ziglar, 1926 – 2012; American Author, Salesperson, and Motivational Speaker)

So don't run away from challenges; embrace them. It is life calling forth from you that which is deposited in you. Just like there cannot be any light without darkness, there cannot be growth without challenges.

Shut your ears when people tell you that you can't do something; don't follow the herd that says it's too difficult. True success is not achieved by listening to the naysayers. *"I've never really been aware of what is said about me, whether it's positive or negative. I ignore it. I've always had the mindset: 'No one can challenge me better than myself'."* (Troy Polamalu; Athlete)

Chapter 17: Be Proactive

"Doing the best at this moment puts you in the best place for the next moment." (Oprah Winfrey; American Media Executive, Talk Show Host, and Philanthropist)

You've carefully set your goals and broken them down into smaller doable actions and now you begin to take daily steps towards the attainment of the goals. What happens when you master the daily steps? Do you continue to follow them or improve upon the steps?

For example, your goal is to build your muscles by lifting 50 pounds of weight for 20 minutes daily. After about 4 weeks of doing the same workout, you could comfortably lift 50 pounds without breaking a sweat. What stops you from increasing the weight and the workout time after such mastery? I'll tell you what: it's sticking to instructions that you've outgrown.

You must realize that working towards your goals means taking progressive steps. You cannot remain in the same spot that you were when you began working on your goals, therefore, you should also continue to raise the bar each time you acclimatize or else you will plateau and stop further progress even though you are still working on your goals.

To be successful at reaching your goals, you must be proactive. You can't stop at what you are told to do.

You must be willing to go further – take the initiative. You can't settle for the minimum requirement if you want to achieve true success. You can churn out 3,000 words per day on your blog, but hey, 1,500 words will do just fine, so why bother, right? Well, guess what: you're never going to make the extraordinary blogger's list with that attitude.

I mentioned this earlier but I guess it's worth mentioning again: you have to be willing to stretch yourself beyond the ordinary, the norm, and the minimum requirement if you want to reap outstanding results.

You have to bid farewell to passiveness and become active. Go on the offense as far as working towards your goal is concerned. Here's what you can begin to do right now:

- Reach out to people who have achieved what you are attempting to do and ask questions that can move you forward.

- Offer to help others who are coming behind you. You learn more by teaching others.

- Don't stop at what you were told. Do your research and make recommendations. It positions you as a sort of authority in your field.

To be proactive also means you think ahead and leave no stone unturned. You are prepared for any eventuality. Stephen R. Covey sums it up beautifully when he said, *"Proactive people carry their own weather with them!"*

Please don't be fooled into thinking that being proactive means that you've got everything under control; because you don't. Things can still go south in spite of your best preparations. In fact, you can fail in an inexplicable way even after you've done the best you think you can do. But failure is an inescapable part of success. Do not let a temporary setback define you. *"Remember that failure is an event, not a person,"* says Zig Ziglar.

"The people who get on in this world are the people who get up and look for the circumstances they want, and, if they can't find them, make them." (George Bernard Shaw, 1856 – 1950; Irish Playwright and Political Activist)

Chapter 18: Measuring Your Progress

"The lessons from business and sports apply to your life; you can't succeed unless you measure the right things and do something about what you learn from the measurement to bring you closer to achieving your goal." (Jerry Bruckner; Author)

How well have you performed with respect to your various goals in the last 24 hours, week, or month? You cannot honestly answer that if you have not measured your progress. The question is: are your goals measurable?

If you do not set goals in specific ways, it becomes impossible to measure your progress. How on God's green earth can you ever manage what you can't measure? How do you know if you are moving forward, standing still, going backwards, or going completely off track? *"You can't manage what you can't measure."* (Peter Drucker, 1909 – 2005; Author, Educator, and Management Consultant). I included that one-line quote from Peter Drucker just in case you prefer to read that idea from a man who's arguably one of the greatest management theorists of all time.

Comparisons

The biggest disservice you can do to yourself is to compare your progress to another person's. First of all, do you know their "why?" Do you know their value system? And even if you do know their inner purpose and their value system, what has that got to do with you?

You are a unique individual, completely different from any other human being and you have a completely different set of "whys." It doesn't serve you to compare your progress to anyone – not even your mentor! Emulating positive traits, habits, and characters is good, but comparing the grounds you have covered to another person's progress is counterproductive.

Look at it this way: if in your comparison with another person, you come to the conclusion (based on your biased assessment) that you have progressed a lot farther than them, does that make you a better person than the other? You are either going to feel more important than the other person or you'll feel pity for them for not making as much progress as you. Both of these are unhelpful to you and the other person. In the unlikely event that you do not feel more important or feel pity for the other person, you'll feel neutral about the comparison, making it effectively useless, to begin with. What's the point in comparing two values and then not making an informed decision?

But then, if in your assessment of another person (which is biased of course), you come to the conclusion that they have progressed farther than you have, you'll either feel bad and less important about yourself or feel pity for yourself. Both of which are not healthy for you and your self-worth. If you feel neutral about not measuring up to the other person, then what's the point of the comparison?

I have said all of this just to say it is absolutely unnecessary to compare your progress to another person's. *"Don't measure your progress using someone else's ruler."* (Binyamin Mughal; Social Media Analyst)

Your focus and attention should simply be on the best you can do with the abilities that you have. Whether the next person is moving forward, standing still, or running backward at 200km/h shouldn't be your concern! *"True success is attained only through the satisfaction of knowing you did everything within the limits of your ability to become the very best that you are capable of being."* (John Wooden, 1910 – 2010; UCLA Basketball Head Coach)

Even if your progress is slow by your estimation, never compare your progress with another person's;stop comparing altogether. *"I am a slow walker, but I never walk back."* (Abraham Lincoln, 1809 – 1865; 16th President of the United States of America)

Measuring your progress tells you if you are steadily heading towards your goals or if you have drifted off the right track. So, while you are eagerly burrowing through the rocks and mountains in the pursuit of your goals, take the time to occasionally measure your progress. You'll know when to pause and take a quick breather, when to double your effort, and when to do a complete u-turn. *"Progress means getting nearer to the place you want to be. And if you have taken a wrong turn, then to go forward does not get you any nearer. If you are on the wrong road, progress means doing an about-turn and walking back to the right road; and in that case, the man who turns back soonest is the most progressive man."* (C. S. Lewis, 1898 – 1963; British Writer and Lay Theologian)

Do This

Once a week or daily (if that is convenient):

- Go through your journal from the previous week or day and see where you were.

- Note the progress you have made so far from the previous week or day.

- Give yourself a pat on the back for even the smallest progress. Pop some champagne if that's your idea of a pat on the back. Strike that out if your goal is to completely stop alcohol consumption! The point is, most people tend to be sterner about their slip-ups than to celebrate their successes.

- Identify places that require adjustment and course correct accordingly. By course correct, I mean take practical steps to correct your mistakes instead of whining in regret. The more time you waste in regret, the more negative your focus tends to become. Remember, "*You don't make progress by standing on the sidelines, whimpering and complaining. You make progress by implementing ideas.*" (Shirley Chisholm, 1924 – 2005; American Politician, Educator, and Author.)

- Tweak areas where you find yourself constantly hitting a brick wall.

The last step is very important. If you have always stumbled using a particular method, consider changing tactics. If you have read something somewhere (even if it is in this book) or you have been advised to do something in a particular way and it just doesn't seem to work for you, tweak it. There are many ways you can follow to arrive at your goal so don't keep bumping your head against a wall if something is not working. If you keep repeating the same thing and failing, you'll soon tire yourself out and either give up or become stagnated. "*There are many ways of going forward, but only one way of standing still.*" (Franklin D. Roosevelt, 1882 – 1945; 32nd President of the United States of America)

Chapter 19: A Moving Target

"When you aim for perfection, you discover it's a moving target." (George Fisher, 1887 – 1972; Archbishop of Canterbury from 1945 to 1961)

Have you ever felt depressed just by remembering that you once had a desire you couldn't achieve? Well, you are not alone; a lot of people have felt and are still feeling that way so much that they shudder each time they hear the words, "setting goals." It reminds them of their failed attempts at trying to reach something they now see as a source of frustration.

Why bother setting goals when it only makes you feel awful about yourself? What's the point?

Perhaps the problem is not with the goals but with our concept of what our goals are. Maybe if we start asking the right questions, it would lead us to the right answers. So, what is a goal to begin with? If we do not really understand what goals are we may be chasing the wind and tire ourselves out in the process. The best of our efforts in the pursuit of something that is not worthwhile is wasted effort. *"There is nothing quite so useless as doing with great efficiency, something that should not be done at all."* (Peter Drucker, 1909 – 2005; Author, Educator, and Management Consultant)

Let's Define a Goal

A goal is a desired result. It is a specific experience or outcome that is time-bound and can be measured.

Okay, now that we've defined what a goal is, I'd like you to do this simple exercise:

1. Bring out your goal book.

2. Go through the goals you've written down for yourself (including those that really give you the jitters!).

3. Ask yourself: does this goal fit into the definition above? Is it specific, time-bound, and measurable? Or is it an open-ended desire?

The aim of this exercise is to help you identify and separate those desires that are concrete goals from those that are not true goals. When you have completed this exercise, list out the desires that are not specific, and categorize them as your ideals.

Let's Define an Ideal

An ideal is a concept that holds the idea of perfection

which is desirable but may not become a reality.

See the difference? One (goal) is specific and measurable; the other (ideal) is simply a desirable concept. In other words, ideals exist only in your imagination. They are not real but can be made real if concrete goals are set in such a way that can lead to their actualization.

Goals and ideals are very different but a whole lot of people confuse the two and this confusion is the actual source of frustration and dispiritedness that many people associate with unfulfilled desires.

An Ideal Is A Moving Target

The problem with trying to catch up with a moving target is that you can never reach it. The more you try to reach it, the farther away from you it goes. But, that is also its advantage. It is not stagnant, therefore, it causes you to reach for greater heights. However, if you do not understand this, you'll continue to beat yourself up for not reaching a moving target.

Your ideal is a moving target. "*I'd like to live a wealthy lifestyle*" is an ideal – a good one at that. But it is not attainable because it is not measurable. How do you define wealthy lifestyle? Wealthy by what standard? Wealthy is just a relative term which is a springboard from where you should set specific, measurable, and time-bound goals.

You can measure goals, but you cannot measure ideals. And if you try to measure an ideal, you usually end up unhappy and frustrated that you are not making any significant progress. The truth is that whatever progress you make is actually insignificant when compared or measured against your moving target because, as I've said before, the more you take steps towards it, the farther away from you it goes.

So, understand the difference so that you stop chasing your own shadows and causing yourself grief in the process.

How then, should we measure the progress we make towards our goals? That is the focus of the next chapter.

Chapter 20: Measure In The Right

Direction

"*Have no fear of perfection – you'll never reach it.*" (Salvador Dali, 1904 – 1989; Spanish Surrealist)

There's a tricky way to lure a chicken into its newly built coop. By leaving a trail of grains that lead all the way into an open hen house, you can get a chicken to follow the track into its coop. That's similar to giving a fish bait to nibble on while you cleverly catch it.

I do not intend to teach you the art of catching animals; my farming skills may be a far cry from perfect, but there's a lesson to be learned here. You will begin to release some emotional hurt if you start seeing your ideals as baits that cleverly "lure" you into more performance, more stretching of yourself, and becoming a better version of yourself. In this regard, your ideal is an excellent growth tool.

However, when you measure your progress in the direction of baits that are cleverly designed to not have any end in sight, you are setting yourself up for frustration. The direction which many people measure progress leaves them unhappy. You may feel you are not making any headway because you are measuring in the wrong direction.

The right way to measure is backward from where you currently are to where you started from. But most of us measure forward from where we are towards our ideal. This is a recipe for frustration!

When you measure yourself against your specific goals instead of your ideals, you can see the actual progress (or otherwise) you have made. You can then properly appraise how well you are performing. You may need to adjust and tweak one or two methods and techniques to improve your progress, but all that will not be possible if your attention is on a moving target.

The Proper Use of Your Ideal

As a yardstick for measuring your progress, your ideal is a poor benchmark to use. The proper use of ideals can be summed up as follows:

1. Ideals are meant to stimulate a positive emotional response from you like positive anticipation and excitement.

2. Ideals spur you to create concrete, time-bound goals that help you strive towards the ideal.

3. Ideals keep you wanting more. Since they are

moving targets, they keep calling forth more from within you.

In effect, if you use your ideal properly, you are constantly becoming a better person as your ideal continues to be refined. This is how to use the elusive future to your advantage.

"We reinterpret or reconstruct our memory in light of what our mental set is in the present. In this sense, it is more accurate to say the present causes the meaning of the past, than it is to say that the past causes the meaning of the present." (Dr. Brent Slife; Clinical Psychologist)

Chapter 21: Connecting To

Abundance

"*When you are grateful, fear disappears and abundance appears.*" (Tony Robbins; Author, Life Coach, and Philanthropist)

Do you feel tired when you read or hear stuff like, "*strive to attain your goals,*" "*stretch yourself beyond your comfort zone,*" "*don't settle for less,*" and all those other yarns geared at motivating you to go further? If you do, you are not alone. Sometimes, it can be quite overwhelming to take in all those motivational talks. It's as if suddenly, someone just dropped the weight of the entire world on your shoulders. "*You mean I have to wake up every day and do all of these mental exercises? Continuously? Forever? No end in sight? Phew! That's one helluva uphill task!*" Yes, it can feel that way sometimes.

This is why you'll need all the support you can get, and what better support system to rely on than one which comes from a source that is constantly available. As creepy as this may sound, you are more than meets the eye. If you recognize this and tap into the part of you that is far beyond flesh and bones, you will be able to access the support you need to help you achieve your goals. I'm not going to bore you with some spiritual mumbo jumbo and go on and on about how you can theoretically tap into some source of abundance. Rather, I'm going to share with you some useful practical steps on how to connect the abundance that lies within you.

The Source Within You

If you can dream it, it already is possible. If it were not a possibility, you would not even have the desire or dream, to begin with. It is rather narrow thinking to assume that the desires which stem from deep within you are purely driven by selfishness. No matter how hard you try to stop them, desires will spring forth from you. Do you doubt that? Go ahead, give it your best shot! And while you are at it, you can ask the Tibetan monks in the Himalayas how well they have been able to subdue all their desires.

There is a source within you from which desires come from. That source is unstoppable. Fighting it is like swimming upstream against a strong current that is flowing downstream; you will just tire yourself out unnecessarily. Doing so is a sure path to frustration. Because as long as you are alive, events must call forth desires from you. Honor the call and chase your dreams. *"Honor your desire for a new life. Say yes to the small inklings of interest and curiosity that present themselves each day."* (Lynn A. Robinson;

One of America's Leading Experts on Intuition)

It is the desires within you that you write down in the form of goals. So, when I refer to desires, I am also referring to your goals. When you make it your life purpose to stay true to your deepest desires, thus, seeking the purpose – the "why" – behind your goals, you will align yourself with the source from which those desires spring from. This simply means you would have opened up yourself to receive insights, creative ideas, short-cuts, tips, and tricks, plus an entire world of new knowledge and skill set to effectively bring your goals to fruition. *"He who lives in harmony with himself lives in harmony with the universe."* (Marcus Aurelius, 121 AD – 180 AD; Roman Emperor and Stoic Philosopher)

Don't Feel Tired Or Overwhelmed

Recognizing and acknowledging that your goals are simply life eager for fuller expression will remove the overwhelming feeling that many people have when they consider all the things they have to do in order to attain their goals and dream lifestyle. Understand that if the wherewithal to achieve your goals is not feasible, the source within you would not cause the stimulation of that desire.

Here's an example of what I mean.

The caveman would not have desired to travel by air like birds because there was no means for that to be actualized in his days. The source within him did not have any support system available to help him in his attainment of that goal at his evolutionary level. But when the wherewithal became available due to evolution, the Wright Brothers conceived the idea of flying as a faster means of transportation. In other words, life was seeking a fuller way of expression with regard to transportation.

So, quit complaining and being overwhelmed by the vastness or enormity of your goals. You can do it, that's why you have that desire. Attach the positive emotions of excitement and anticipation to your goals and you will summon the internal support system that is always readily available for you. *"If you always attach positive emotions to the things you want, and never attach negative emotions to the things you don't, then that which you desire most will invariably come your way."* (Matt D. Miller)

Okay, as much as I love positive thinking and the corresponding positive feeling that should accompany those thoughts, I equally like to come out of the thought-world and take actual physical steps that will cause the actualization of my goals. So, what happens next after conceptually acknowledging the availability of an internal support system as well as attaching positive emotions to your goals or desires? That is the subject of our next chapter.

Chapter 22: Increasing Your Connection to The Inner Source of Abundance

"As long as we remain vigilant at building our internal abundance—an abundance of integrity, an abundance of forgiveness, an abundance of service, an abundance of love—then external lack is bound to be temporary." (Marianne Williamson; Author, Lecturer, and Activist)

You've identified your goals. You've also acknowledged that it is very possible to achieve them. This acknowledgment creates excitement and positive emotions about your goals. Now, you need to increase and strengthen your connection to your inner source of abundance by developing the habit of practicing the following:

Practice Gratitude

Get a journal and write in it the things you are

grateful for on a daily basis. These should include insights about your goals, the steps you have taken in the direction of your goals, as well as physical and material possessions you have. *"Summoning gratitude is a sure way to get our life back on track. Opening our eyes to affirm gratitude grows the garden of our inner abundance, just as standing close to a fire eventually warms our heart."* (Alexandra Katehakis; Clinical Director of Center for Healthy Sex, and Author)

If you truly want to enjoy the full benefits of gratitude, allow yourself to truly feel the emotion of what you are writing in your gratitude journal. Don't just pour out empty emotionless words on the pages of your journal. Feel them as you write them.

The practice of gratitude is not just some New Age stuff or religious practice. It is a scientifically proven method of improving your overall psyche. When you engage in this practice, you open yourself to physical, spiritual, psychological, and health benefits. Here are some of the benefits:

- Gratitude boosts your creativity and by extension, your career.

- Gratitude boosts your self-esteem; you will begin to see yourself differently as a better and more confident person.

- Gratitude can quickly get you back on your feet after facing challenges.

- Gratitude decreases your chances of envious competition, mindless comparison, and feeling jealous about any other person's good fortune.

- Gratitude develops your charisma.

- Gratitude gives you a firm grip on your emotions.

- Gratitude has a way of making you want to exercise more which in turn improves your energy levels.

- Gratitude helps you draw closer to achieving your goals by consistently noticing the small improvements. The more you notice these improvements and feel grateful about them, the more your brain wants to experience the good feeling that comes with gratitude, thus, propelling you to take more steps and notice more improvements.

- Gratitude improves your outlook on life, making you more optimistic about life in general.

- Gratitude improves your relationship with colleagues, friends, family, and spouse.

- Gratitude leads to inner calm, peace, and tranquility. With inner peace comes better functioning of your physiology and a healthier you.

- Gratitude makes you a happier person because your focus is on the positive aspects of your life. Remember whatever you focus on expands in your life.

- Gratitude makes you more likable. Other people warm up to you.

- Gratitude makes you see the good in all situations. Your attention is deliberately held riveted on the good in all persons and situation.

- Gratitude shifts your focus away from egocentrism and self-centeredness.

- Gratitude strengthens your spirituality making you more connected to the source within you. You become more intuitive.

- When practiced at night or just before sleep, gratitude helps you enjoy quality sleep.

Practice Mastery

One of the greatest mistakes that you will make in the pursuit of your goals is to chase after the external signs of success. The cars, jewelry, abs and curves, accolades, promotions, and all the other stuff that represent physical success will come to you if you give your undivided attention to the mastery of what you do. *"People who become 'elite' at what they do aren't striving to be 'elite' just to join some special club. They take great joy and satisfaction in the pursuit of mastery, and they compete against themselves, not others."* (Justine Musk; Canadian Author)

So, what is it that you want to achieve, and what is it that you know how to do or need to learn how to do in order to achieve that thing? Focus on becoming good at that thing and success will naturally follow you.

Joseph Campbell puts it beautifully:

"Follow your bliss. If you do follow your bliss, you put yourself on a kind of track that has been there all the while waiting for you, and the life you ought to be living is the one you are living. When you can see that, you begin to meet people who are in the field of your bliss, and they open the doors to you. I say, follow your bliss and don't be afraid, and doors will open where you didn't know they were going to be. If you follow your bliss, doors will open for you that wouldn't have opened for anyone else." (Joseph Campbell, 1904 – 1987; American Professor of Literature)

I have read and heard a lot of debate about following your bliss. What do you say to someone who says playing Candy Crush is their bliss? Does that sound like something that can translate into success in the world we live in? I seriously doubt that! However, that debate largely stems from the misconception about what bliss is.

According to Sarah Rudell Beach, bliss simply means *"that which brings you contentment through doing good for others"* (n.d.). This means your bliss is not just what you like doing or what you have passion for. It is doing something that bestows some form of goodness to others. Something that is beneficial to both you and others in some meaningful and purposeful way.

So, go ahead and learn that skill or perfect what you already know how to do. Improve upon your work, master your skills, and become an expert at what you do. This is one way to increase the connection to your inner abundance.

Note that when you follow your bliss, it can lead you to many paths. There is not just one form of bliss cut out for you. There are several passions and by extension, several things, you can gain mastery on.

I like this speech delivered by Steven Spielberg because it sums it up nicely:

"When you have a dream, it doesn't often come at you screaming in your face: 'This is who you are. This is what you must be for the rest of your life.' Sometimes a dream almost whispers. And I've always said to my kids: The hardest thing to listen to – your instincts, your human personal intuition – always whispers, it never shouts. Very hard to hear. So you have to, every day of your lives, be ready to hear what whispers in your ear. It very rarely

shouts. And if you can listen to the whisper, and if it tickles your heart, and it's something you think you want to do for the rest of your life, then that is going to be what you do for the rest of your life and we will benefit from everything you do." (Steven Spielberg; American Filmmaker)

Practice Tapping Into Your Genius

Believe it or not (I do hope you believe it), you are a genius. There is no such thing as a useless human being. It may not appear to you that you are a genius but you do have all the potential in you. You were born with it.

Even great scientist Albert Einstein never believed he could amount to anything, at least his childhood proved that much to be true. He was naturally slow in learning how to speak. But by tapping into his genius, he became one of the greatest physicists to walk the surface of this planet.

Here are practical ways to tap into your genius. Practice these things as often as you can.

1. **Find Excitement**: As we grow up into adults, many of us outgrew the feeling of excitement. We forgot how to get excited about things so much that we are amazed when we see kids get excited over little things.

Thankfully, you as an adult can still get back that feeling of excitement. But why is that necessary? It is necessary because excitement changes your chemistry; your mind, body, and soul. It lifts your energy level and allows you to tap into creativity.

2. **Get Some Movement**: What probably comes to your mind when you are bored and tired is to lie down and rest, right? Great. What if you took boredom as a sign to get active? It is your body telling you that you are out of alignment with your true self. Go for a walk in nature or do some physical exercise to get your creative juices flowing.

3. **Seek Silence**: Form the habit of "going into the silence" or meditating even if it is for 10 minutes. And when I say meditation, I do not mean that you must necessarily cross your legs and sit in a lotus position humming or chanting mantras! What I mean by meditation or silence is to simply be by yourself and take the time to contemplate things. Pause all the busyness and activities of your life and give thought to just one thing. You are giving your inner genius the opportunity to sneak out and pop some creative thoughts into your calm mind.

4. **Seek Joy**: Give your attention to things that bring you joy and exclude from your life those things that are a source of pain and sorrow.

The more joyful experiences and people you allow in your life, the healthier your state of mind, and the more your genius can come to fore.

5. **Team Up**: You are not an island – no man or woman is. Seek out people who share in your bliss, your passion; people who are like-minded and collaborate. Share ideas, ask the right questions, and you'll be amazed by what you can collectively achieve.

Chapter 23: How To Exponentially Increase Your Success

"It's not the big things that add up in the end; it's the hundreds, thousands, or millions of little things that separate the ordinary from the extraordinary." (Darren Hardy; American Author, Motivational Speaker, and former Publisher of Success Magazine)

Have you ever experienced the compound effect of anything? You most certainly have, unless of course, you are an infant. In which case, you won't be reading this! Little bits of action or inactions can amount to a significant difference over time. For example, you do not become obese by eating unhealthily just one time. It takes consistent repetition over time before you become obese. However, because you usually won't set a goal to become obese, you hardly see all the hard work that goes into becoming obese. You were merely enjoying fast foods, junk foods, and foods that weren't suitable for you without considering the long-term effect of your actions.

The same thing applies to something positive like practicing a few minutes of mindfulness on a daily basis. It doesn't appear as if any change is taking place in you but over time, your general outlook on life is calmer, more composed, deliberate, and you no longer live from a place of reaction.

A compound effect can either be negative or positive. You have the choice to use it to your advantage and exponentially increase your success. Here's how:

Be Deliberate About Your Day

We all have 24 hours allotted to us in one day; that's no news. What's news, however, is that some people can produce in that amount of time what it will take others a whole year! And why is that so? It is simply because we all use our time differently. Here are a few suggestions to help you leverage your 24-hour period.

1. Form the habit of waking up one hour earlier than usual. The compounding effect of this singular habit will blow your mind. This habit gives you ample time to practice mindfulness, think up creative ideas, and go into your day without being rushed. When you wake up just in time for your daily activities, you tend to just rush through your morning and into your day. You hardly have time to contemplate on the things that are important to you. If you do not give your mind quality time to think, how can it come up with quality ideas? *"Lose an hour in the morning, and you will spend all*

day looking for it." (Richard Whately, 1787 – 1863; English Rhetoric and Economist)

2. Form the habit of spending a quality evening before going to bed. It will amount to near waste if you start your day right but end it wrong. Most people spend their evenings in front of the TV or chatting on social media until late into the night. Now, I'm not suggesting you shouldn't watch TV or use social media, but you will do well to follow the suggestions in chapter 8 about unplugging.

Manage Your Energy

Schedule your activities to fall during the hours you are normally high on energy. If the morning hours are more productive for you, prioritize your most important activities to fit into that window. This shifts your attention from merely trying to manage your time to deliberately designing your day to suit your energy level.

Reduce The Items On Your To-Do List

This may sound counterintuitive, but it is true. You

see, we live in a society where *"I'm busy"* is worn like some sort of medal. *"Just because you are doing a lot more, doesn't mean you're getting a lot more done."* (Denzel Washington; American Actor, Movie Director, and Producer)

Take a long hard look at your daily to-do list and strike out things that are not essential. Keep your daily activities as simple as can be. Having a long list of things to do on your list is a clear indication that your mind is busy, crowded, and there's no room for creative ideas to flow. Occupying yourself with too much activity in one day doesn't guarantee productivity. So, if you are someone who usually has a to-do list that is full, take a deep breath, go through your list, and identify the top 5 most important things that absolutely have to be done that day. Focus only on those things to the exclusion of the rest until you have completed them.

"Simplicity boils down to two steps: Identify the essential. Eliminate the rest." (Leo Babauta; Journalist, Author, and Blogger)

Be Patient

The word "patience" doesn't exist in many people's vocabulary. They just can't stand it, so they simply took out that word from their mental dictionary. *"I want results and I want them now!*" That's what most people's behavior says.

They hate it when people like Malcolm Gladwell, author of *Outliers*, say it takes 10,000 hours of practice to become good at whatever you do. They immediately go, "*What? Who has that much time? I'll better shelve the whole idea of pursuing this goal.*"

Well, you cannot become an expert in your field, or become a better version of yourself without a willingness to "do the time." Although, whether 10,000 hours is the magic number for expertise to be achieved or not is debatable, the point is, it takes time for the results you seek to show up.

When people engage in harmful habits, the negative effect doesn't show up immediately, which is why they keep doing it. But why do we expect the immediate positive effect to show up when we begin to engage in positive habits? If you were to lose one tooth each time you engage in a counterproductive habit, you most definitely will not continue in that harmful habit, or else sooner or later, you would lose all your teeth and probably your tongue too! But because there is no immediate visible negative repercussion, you continue to ignore the consequences and indulge just one more time. However, with positive behavior you expect money in your account immediately, the excess weight to magically vanish, the promotion to come tomorrow morning, and the muscles and abs to show up already!

The reason you do not have patience is because you are constantly checking up on the seed you planted and screaming at it "*grow!*" This reminds me of the donkey in the animation movie *Shrek 2* where the donkey (voiced by Eddie Murphy) kept asking Shrek (Mike Myers) and Princess Fiona (Cameron Diaz) "*are we there yet?*" on their way to the kingdom of Far-Far-Away. (You should watch that movie if you haven't.)

The point is this: in your quest for results, as your ideals call forth more desires from you, and as you strive to reach your goals, remember that it will take some time before the effect of your daily actions bears meaningful fruits.

"A daily routine built on good habits and disciplines separates the most successful among us from everyone else. A routine is exceptionally powerful." (Darren Hardy)

Chapter 24: Can You Be Driven

And Happy?

"Be driven, be focused, but enjoy every moment, because it only happens once." (Alicia Keys; Musician, Actress, and Philanthropist)

Here's a quick tip: chasing success and happiness is like chasing the wind; you can never catch up with the wind. Both success and happiness are byproducts of who you become in the process of gunning for your goals.

But can you be happy and driven at the same time?

We live in a society where happiness and striving for greater heights seems to be mutually exclusive. You either accept life the way it has been doled out to you and be happy with it or you postpone your happiness until such a time when you have accomplished all of your goals (or at least the important ones).

We hear things like, "be content with what you have; that's the secret to true happiness!" While this may sound like great advice to some, to others, it is another way of settling for mediocrity.

On the other hand, we hear motivational statements like, "Don't settle for less. Be dissatisfied with being average. Aim for the top and when you get there aim farther!" This line of talk may sound motivating for some, but to others, it is being ungrateful for what you currently have.

It seems you cannot be driven and at the same time happy. Or can you?

Short answer: yes you can!

Now for the long answer.

There is absolutely no reason why you should postpone your happiness until you achieve certain results in life. When you read books about goals, there is a tendency to fall into thinking that there is an end where you will have to get to before you become satisfied. But the truth is that there is no end, there never has been and there never will be. So if you keep delaying your happiness until you get to the end, you may as well forget about being happy. You are simply chasing the wind!

Conversely, there is absolutely no reason why you should settle for less than you can be, do, and have. You are not placed on this earth for mediocrity! You are here to be a shining example of what is humanly possible with your gifts and talent. It would be rather unfortunate to go to the grave with what would have advanced life on planet earth. "Let us live so that when we come to die, the undertaker will be sorry!" Mark Twain, 1835 – 1910; Writer, Entrepreneur, and Publisher)

Let the undertaker be sorry when they come to bury you because there is nothing left to be buried than human flesh. It would be a shame to be buried with untapped possibilities! "The graveyard is the richest place on earth, because it is here that you will find all the hopes and dreams that were never fulfilled, the books that were never written, the songs that were never sung, the inventions that were never shared, the cures that were never discovered, all because someone was too afraid to take that first step, keep with the problem, or determined to carry out their dream." (Les Brown; Motivational Speaker, Author)

You can be happy while working towards your goals. You don't have to sacrifice one for the other. The two are not mutually exclusive. You don't have to settle for less in order to be happy; neither do you have to give up being happy just because you are chasing after your goals.

Chapter 25: Success and

Achievement

"You are not here merely to make a living. You are here in order to enable the world to live more amply, with greater vision, with a finer spirit of hope and achievement. You are here to enrich the world, and you impoverish yourself if you forget the errand." (Woodrow Wilson, 1856 – 1924; 28th President of the United States of America from 1913 to 1921)

Why does it seem like becoming successful can cause you to become unhappy? There are lots of people who are successful but aren't happy at all. This may leave you wondering: is the pursuit of my goals really worth it if it will lead me to unhappiness?

To answer that, let us closely look at these two words: "success" and "achievement." Both words are used interchangeably but they are not quite the same.

Success is the good feeling that you have about your progress or performance with regards to your goals. Why you are doing what you are doing and how well you are doing it is entirely up to you and that is what success is about. It is a subjective feeling. That means, only you can truly define what success means to you.

It is your standard, your yardstick, and your measurement.

Achievement, on the other hand, is the measure of what you have actually accomplished. It is not a subjective feeling but an objective measure of the milestones you've covered thus far.

Now, here's what all this boils down to:

- People who you think are successful but unhappy are merely high achievers. They have achieved far beyond the "ordinary" folks would, yet they are not happy because they are not truly successful.

- External indicators of success do not necessarily translate to true success. You may have achieved the perfect body shape, your bank account may have become fat and shapeless, your garage may need to be expanded because of the fleet of cars, and you may have finally stolen the heart of that handsome or beautiful partner, yet you are a complete wreck on the inside!

- True success is a feeling of inward happiness and can be sustained because its focus remains constantly on your "why."

- Achievement shifts the focus from your "why" to the seeking external validation.

Don't get this twisted: you cannot become successful

without achieving things. But you definitely can achieve things without being successful. It's a subtle difference, but it makes all the difference in the world.

Do This

- Every day, find some 5 minutes out of your busy schedule to say "thank you" for the things you have accomplished. It doesn't matter who or what you are grateful to; God, yourself, some higher power, or whatever belief system you subscribe to. The bottom line is to be genuinely grateful for your achievements. This practice shifts your attention from blindly burrowing through one mountain of achievement to the other in the pursuit of personal aggrandizement, to recognizing the reason why you are actually accomplishing your goals.

- Whenever possible, sincerely and openly acknowledge the help you get in the course of your achievements. You are connecting with your essence in that process instead of your ego.

- Practice anonymous giving. From your numerous accomplishments, give out praise, commendation, recommendation, cash, knowledge, and so on. *"When you learn, teach. When you get, give."* (Maya Angelou, 1928 – 2014; Poet and Civil Rights Activist) It would be great if you can find a way to do this anonymously. For one, it makes it more fun, and secondly, it helps you to focus on others too. And when I say give, I do not mean to suggest that you give only to those you consider as needy. Let your giving be without bias.

Chapter 26: Sustaining Success and Happiness

"*Our capacity to draw happiness from aesthetic objects or material goods in fact seems critically dependent on our first satisfying a more important range of emotional or psychological needs, among them the need for understanding, for love, expression and respect.*" (Alain De Botton; British Philosopher and Author)

Now that you know that there's a world of difference between achievement and success, how do you ensure that you maintain the feeling of success over a long time? How do you continue being happy after you have reached a milestone or even achieved a huge goal?

You see, succeeding for the first time may cause you to become flooded with some serious wave of happiness. But after the several wins, that feeling of happiness that comes with being successful seems to gradually die off. Why is that? It is because of something you probably must have learned or heard of in high school: the law of diminishing returns.

The Law of Diminishing Returns

This is a fundamental economic principle that simply means that something becomes less valuable the more you get it. This principle goes beyond economics to every aspect of human life.

The more times you accomplish something, the less excitement you get from it because it's no longer new to you. Over time, it may become a chore, a bore, or even a source of dissatisfaction for you. This is what pushes people from becoming successful to becoming high achievers. When you lose the vision of your purpose, you become obsessed with blindly achieving more to satisfy some innate crave within you. And because that inward craving cannot be satisfied by the attainment of one goal, you get stuck in an unhappy state of forever chasing after achievements in the guise of chasing success.

To drive home the point, here are a few examples:

- If you are struggling to get by and you somehow got creative and landed $10,000 in your bank account, you will most likely be excited and happy. The first time you hit the $1 million dollar mark, you will definitely feel very happy and accomplished. Making $10,000 after that may not feel as much of an accomplishment because you've *"been there, done that!"*

- Losing 25 pounds in your first few weeks of working out may excite you, but staying at 85 pounds over time will make it feel like a bore.

- Winning a championship for the very first time is an amazing feeling. However, after a series of winning streaks, the juice is already squeezed out of the feeling.

So what can be done to sustain the feeling of happiness and success as you go after your goals?

Do This

- Ruminate over your purpose every once in a while to keep it fresh in your mind.

- Fall completely in love with the process of fulfilling your purpose.

- Continually refine your purpose with every goal you accomplish. Use the accomplishment as an occasion to take a clearer look at your moving target – your ideal.

If you do not fall deeply in love with the process of

fulfilling your purpose – your "why" – you will lose your vision and begin to chase achievements that leave you empty. Sustaining happiness and the feeling of success depends entirely on how deeply you are in love with why you do the things you do. Ah! Don't you just love falling in love! *"Doing what you like is freedom. Liking what you do is happiness."* (Frank Tyger, 1929 – 2011; Editorial Cartoonist and Columnist)

In other words, you can be successful and happy at the same time if you keep the love of what you do alive. Loving the process of physical exercise will guarantee that you'll become successful at your weight loss or bodybuilding goal while being happy along the way. Falling in love with the practice of providing for your family and loved ones will bring out the best in you. At the same time, it will keep you going before, during, and after the achievement of your goal. You will generally become a better person who attracts success. *"Success is something you attract by the person you become."* (Jim Rohn, 1930 – 2009; Entrepreneur, Author, Motivational Speaker)

These People Fell In Love With Their "Why"

Why doesn't Warren Buffett simply quit investing? Why is Mark Zuckerberg still working? Why is

Richard Branson not tired yet? Why are these men still doing what they are doing even after being hugely successful and very happy? They have achieved far more than the average Joe, yet they are still at work as if they just began today! I don't think it's because of the money – they have truckloads of the green stuff already, so much so that they possibly cannot exhaust even if they stopped bringing in more.

They are doing what they are doing because of the love they have for it. The money motivation died off a long time ago but their "whys" are still very much alive.

Serena Williams and Nick Saban are all still actively engaging in their various sports activities. Is it for the money, for the fame, to get to the top of their sporting career, or for the love of what they do? These people have fallen head over heels in love with what they do so much so that they live and breathe the sport.

David Goggins and Jack Lalanne are not working out because they have a goal of losing weight. They have fallen in love with exercising for decades and are still at it as if their lives depended on it.

Bottom Line

Loving what you do means focusing on the process. The process of getting to your goals must be your focus and not just the goals themselves. "*Success is assured when a person fears the pain of regret more than the pain of the process."* (Orrin Woodward; Author)

The law of diminishing returns is inescapable if you do not have a stronger motivation beyond the mere achievement of goals. This is why many of the people we call truly successful have multimillion dollar foundations that support different causes. They have gone beyond mere achievement for the sake of the ego to success for the sake of fulfilling an inner sense of purpose.

"Life is a journey, and if you fall in love with the journey, you will be in love forever." (Peter Hagerty)

Conclusion

Do not lose hope if your goals seem beyond your immediate reach. I will suggest that you should take that as an opportunity to stretch yourself and grow beyond your current phase. If there are no more goals to reach for, then we are dead while living. And if your goals are easy to reach, you are not growing. You're like a healthy normal adult who sets a goal for learning how to walk. That's completely laughable because it doesn't result in growth.

Keep in mind that you have to become a certain type of person in order to attain your goals. It is not just the obtaining of a physical object or attaining of a goal that really matters, but the person you become in the process of pursuing the goal. So, set goals that are bound to make you a better version of yourself than you currently are. As Michael Korda wisely puts it, *"One way to keep momentum going is to have constantly greater goals."*

Do not just read this book as a way to increase your library collection. There is no trophy for the person with the largest collection of books. It is in the reading and application of what is learned that trophies are awarded, fulfillment attained and lives improved. Reading this book alone won't make you double your income, or increase your productivity without you putting in the required effort to succeed.

"Don't let your learning lead to knowledge. Let your learning lead to action." (Jim Rohn)

Make this your go-to book for your personal and professional goal achievements. Read it more than once. Allow it to take effect in your life by applying the suggestions contained in it. You will be all the better for it.

Finally, we may all have different inherent abilities but we do share one resource in common and that is time. Every single individual who has made significant progress in their lives, despite all odds (some whom I've mentioned briefly in this book), have the same 24 hour day period as you. However, the one thing that made them stand out is their ability to structure their time around the things that are most important to them – their goals. If you can do just that, you will go a long way in attaining those things that are dearest to you.

As I bring this book to a close, I'd like to re-echo what Norman Vincent Peale said, *"Believe in yourself! Have faith in your abilities! Without a humble but reasonable confidence in your own powers, you cannot be successful or happy."*